The Life and T[barcode] Roger J Star~ ~~~~

C000061037

By

Roger J Starbuck

Acknowledgements

This book is dedicated to ....

My wife Heather for her encouragement, support and love over the last 45 years

To my son Richard for the front cover design and illustrations

To Kristi McDermott for managing to read my atrocious handwriting and for her word processing talent

To Lucinda Reed for her proof reading skill

Contents

Prologue

My motivation to write this book came largely from the knowledge that we are not that great at writing things down anymore.

The art of letter writing is clearly on the decline and I certainly cannot recall the last letter I wrote!

Photos taken on our mobile phones are often not printed out for future generations to see.

So to my complete surprise many half-forgotten memories have flooded back to me from the inner cobwebs of my mind to create this book.

If I have confused dates, situations and facts, or even totally missed important aspects of my life, this is entirely accidental, please forgive me.

ENJOY!

The Early Years

I spent my entire childhood plus my early twenties living at 9 The Close, Pampisford Road, Purley, Surrey. Our phone number was Uplands 1268 which my Mother always pronounced in a very posh voice! We lived in a semi-detached house that was positioned high up on one side of a U-shaped valley. The other side of the valley had the London to Brighton main railway line, which could only be heard when the wind blew in a certain direction (or that is how my parents chose to describe the background noise). And yes, I can remember the steam trains still running on the electrified lines!

The Valley was known as 'Bomb Alley' during World War II as apparently the RAF planes used to chase the Germans out of London towards the English South Coast, so the Germans tended to drop any spare bombs in their race to get away. We also had Croydon Airport only a mile or so away, which at the time was an RAF base. It was a miracle that we were not all blown to bits!

The Close was a small community of just 12 houses, approached down a steep hill with a very sharp left turn. There was also a roundabout at the end of the no-through road where rose trees grew surrounded by grass.

I had an idyllic childhood in our little Close.

At Number 1 lived Mr and Mrs Potter and their son Stephen. They all spoke with what I considered to be a posh accent. Very occasionally I was allowed to play with Stephen who was several years older than me. He subsequently went to Whitgift School in South Croydon which was, and still is, the elite academic school in the area.

Number 2 had a Mr and Mrs McKinney. I remember Mrs McKinney smiling a great deal at me. I'm not sure if she liked me or if that was her way of closing her front door as quickly as possible. Her husband was tall, thickset and walked with a stick and wore strange blue-tinted glasses. Looking back, he may have been blind, but as a very young lad this thought never crossed my mind.

I am unable to recall the original occupants of Number 3, but for many years Peggy and her daughter were in residence. Peggy was always friendly to my parents (my father may have fancied her?) but she always found the time to chat with me.

At Number 4 there was a very tall guy and his younger brother who was disadvantaged (we used to say a bit mental in those days). Strange that some 20 plus years later we would be destined to live in this very house as a young family. Happy memories!

At Number 5 was the infamous Ida and her 'plain-clothed' policeman husband. He was charming.

The occupants of Number 6 had their front door kicked in. This happened in broad daylight with money stolen from their hallway. It was the only crime ever to hit The Close.

Number 7 had a strange Spanish couple, where the husband always went off to work at exactly the same time each morning, complete with his leather briefcase. We set the time by him. I can still hear the steel heals clicking as he passed Number 9. I had a theory that he was actually a spy as some neighbours said the small front bedroom light stayed on all night, every night! Many years later I remember asking him if he was a spy; they moved a few months later ...

Rene Holmes lived at Number 8, a spinster of this parish who I knew as Auntie Rene. Her garden was almost completely overgrown. I sometimes earned pocket money by attempting to clear a small segment. She was, however, very kind and I recall being invited to tea with my Mother. The house was almost as chaotic as the garden. We had tea and cake.

Auntie Dorrie and her husband Bob lived at Number 10. She was the life and soul of The Close. Dorrie almost lived in our house, always popping in with the shout of 'It's only me!' as she burst in through our back door. My Mother said that she sometimes found her irritating, but Auntie Dorrie did possess the only washing mangle in The Close, so they remained firm friends.

Bob and Dorrie had adopted twins, Gwen and Tim, who must have been in their late teens. I vividly recall Gwen coming around to our house when her Father died. She sat on our stairs sobbing. This may have been the first time that I had seen anyone outwardly grieving.

There were very important people at Number 11, as they were the only household to have a TV! The lucky couple were Reg and Win who also had a maiden aunt, Miss Bryant, living with them.

Oh the excitement when I was invited to see the very first Children's Hour on the BBC. I think it was blessed by a Bishop, which I found a little strange. The main event was 'Rin Tin Tin', which starred an Alsatian dog. I used to avidly look forward to each weekly instalment. Later Miss Bryant died and, as was the custom at the time, she was laid out in her bedroom. I was asked if I would like to pay my respects but the thought of a dead person was just too much for my young mind.

Finally, Number 12 – sadly they will have to remain anonymous, but she was a ballerina with The Royal Ballet Company in London – wow!

Our house was a typical three bed with, in my eyes, seemingly large rooms; which included a separate dining room and lounge. Most of the furniture was called 'utility', as it was manufactured during the war years to help people who had been bombed out of their houses. I particularly remember the sofa which according to my Mother had shrapnel marks, but I never found any!

Outside, the front garden had a severe slope down to the front door. The back garden, which I thought was large, was reached by going down half a dozen steps.

When I was 12, I set up a cricket pitch in the back garden, which must have been about 15 yards at most. No wonder my bowling was always short pitched! My Father sometimes asked me to mow the back lawn, but I usually got away with just my cricket pitch!

I think my parents bought 9 The Close for £500 after being bombed out of their previous house in Shirley, Croydon.

I was meant to have two sisters, but Janet sadly died after just two months in 1940.

After I was born my Mother became pregnant again, but unfortunately fell downstairs and lost her baby girl. I don't remember this but do recall a lady in a white coat (a home help in those far off days) cooking and looking after my Father and myself. My Mother's parents were also at Number 9 during this very sad time. We went by taxi to collect my Mother from hospital, and I remember seeing my grandfather and my Father helping her across the grass towards the car. Looking back maybe I can now see why my 'Mummy' was so domineering and protective of me through my formative years.

Years later while undertaking my Ancestry research, I made contact with one of the Young family (my Mother's maiden name) who by this time were living in Canada. They wanted to make absolutely certain that Janet should always be remembered and placed in the Starbuck Ancestry records. Clearly they must have been very close to my Mother at the time Janet died.

Thinking back as I researched this book, other childhood memories come flooding back. So here goes:

The milkman used to come around every day complete with his horse and cart. The keen gardeners in The Close used to follow on behind the horse with a bucket and spade just in case it 'performed'. Good for the gardens you know!

George, the baker, delivered the bread in his three-wheeled vehicle. (An earlier version of the Only Fools and Horses three-wheeler). You could hear him coming from miles away. His van broke down one Christmas Eve, but he still managed to deliver just before midnight.

The trams terminated at Purley Crossroads. Just imagine the chaos if they still operated at this junction, it has become one of the busiest in the South East. They travelled along the A23 through Croydon and onwards into London, terminating at Elephant and Castle.

My parents went to see the final tram leave Purley in 1951. Thousands came and waved flags, sang and no doubt cried. I was taken on a tram during their final week and remember passengers holding Union Jacks. Although time has shrouded them in nostalgia they were, in reality, rather dangerous. As the lines were just below road level, and situated in the middle of the road, you had to walk halfway across the road to get on or off them!

There was a large Sainsbury's in Purley, where you had to queue up at a different counter for each type of product! It must have taken ages. Woolworths were situated nearby, where after Christmas everything was sold for just one old penny. An excellent way of disposing of all their old rubbish I guess.

Just a few yards down from Woolworths was the 'dog meat' shop. During my teens we had a wired hair terrier dog called 'Taffy'. I think he was a rescue dog. One day I was in the 'dog meat' shop with my lovely Taffy, when the dog was greeted by his name by the shop assistant, "Have you come for your usual bone?"; this explained why Taffy was always going missing from Number 9. Goodness knows how he managed to cross the main roads to the shop, but he somehow survived.

My Mother, like most of the population, did not have a fridge so things were generally kept in the 'scullery', which had been converted from a 'coal cellar'! The coalman used to deliver the coal in sacks slung over his shoulders. He tended to have a very black face and hands and smelt of coal. In order to replace the coal cellar my Father built an alternative made of breezeblocks, which for years was situated around the back, outside the dining room. Uncle Bertie (my Mother's brother) used to say that it would fall down at any minute. Years later my Father (who was as useless as me at building things) would say to Bertie "it's still standing".

I don't think they liked each other that much?

We had an open coal fire, which was lit using a large piece of newspaper held over the fireplace opening to help it draw. I suspect this was rather dangerous, but I can still hear the roar of the flames as the fire ignited. The newspaper often used to catch fire. I remember that we also had a few chimney fires!

I have memories of waking up in the wintertime with frost on the inside of our metal windows. You had to scrape the frost off. This was long before the luxury of double-glazing or, for that matter, central heating.

Tea leaves – not tea bags. Just poured from the teapot via a strainer. This never caught all the leaves, hence tea leaves at the bottom of the cup – some made a living 'reading' the tea leaves – I don't think it was based on scientific theory! There was always a tea cosy placed over the teapot, usually a handmade knitted variety. Come to think of it, the loo roll often had a knitted cover as well!

As a child all summers were perfect weatherwise and I used to play outside with Michael Brown and Alan Drake who both lived on the next road.

Trolley buses ran from Mitcham to Shepherd's Bush passing near West Croydon Station. I have no idea why I sometimes used them, but I did. They ran using overhead wires linked to large poles on each bus. These sometimes fell off so the driver had to reconnect them by using another long pole along with language which was not considered polite.

I used to collect stamps from all parts of the world (nerdy, yes but many of us did the same) and I still have my priceless collection proudly displayed in my stamp album. Very recently I sent photographic evidence of my more 'priceless' stamps to Stanley Gibbons who have a number of specialists only to receive the response that if they found anything of value they would let me know. I never had a reply.

My Mother made a cake to celebrate the Queen's Coronation in 1953. The government had apparently decided that, even though rationing was still in place, each household would receive an extra one pound of sugar and four ounces of margarine.

Yoyos were all the rage, becoming a must have toy for every child. The school playground became a competition as to who would be the Champion.

Snakes and Ladders, Ludo and Monopoly were often played in my house, usually on the dining room table. We had a radio, which was the only source for news, music and comedy programmes. The tuning device on these early models required a very deft hand in order to come up with the 'light' programme, which I guess is now the equivalent of Radio 2 of its day.

There wasn't that much on the radio for us children but I do vividly remember 'Uncle Mac' of the BBC who always signed off with, "Goodnight Children Everywhere". I think it was 6pm at the time; he also presented Children's Favourites every Saturday morning, which for me was often the highlight of my week. For some reason Derek McCulloch (Uncle Mac) was a Croydon Stagers Vice President and sometimes came to our musicals. I asked him on one occasion for his autograph, which he gave me with rather a sullen response. Never liked him much after that!!

My parents, along with most people, had to shop everyday as only a very few people possessed a fridge. The fishmonger on Purley High Street was always visited. I can still remember the piles of ice surrounding the fish.

I think I was a teenager when my parents bought a radiogram where you could listen to a growing number of stations but also play '78' records. My Mother polished the wooden cabinet nearly every day. I listened to Radio Luxembourg, which was the forerunner of the pirate radio stations. The signal was not that great and sometimes dropped out right in the middle of the latest release!

Mount Everest was first conquered in 1953 at around the time of the Queen's Coronation, with a runner dispatched to spread the news to the World.

In South Croydon there was a very small cinema called 'The Classic'. We all went to see the film footage of the Everest ascent along with Pathé News, which was updated every week. The Classic was known as the 'flea pit' but was very art deco with a capacity of only around 100 people. If you visited during an afternoon showing the usherette served cups of tea from a very large metal teapot.

My conversion to films took place on a school visit to see Charles Dickens's 'Great Expectations' at this cinema. Not only did I love the story and the film, but immediately fell in love with Jean Simmons then a beautiful young actress playing the part of Estella. My crush lasted several years.

World War II ration books – you secured both food and clothes via coupons. If you didn't have enough coupons, you didn't get the item. Rations continued after the war until 1954. There was a substantial 'black market' throughout the war.

I remember my 12th birthday party when my Mother, to celebrate the end of rationing, gave everyone cream cakes. No one ate them, largely because we had never experienced or eaten anything like them before. She was so upset, especially as everything was still scarce; they must have cost a bomb.

I also built and kept a slug farm in the garden. I collected hundreds of them, which kind of pleased my parents as the plants were not eaten – well not quite so much.

I had a wigwam in the garden and used to dress up as an Indian, complete with the feather headgear. You can make what you want from that!

To celebrate passing my 11+ (just) I was bought a Tri-ang Electric Train set (it was actually a bribe if I passed!). I still have the train set in the hope that it would by now be worth a small fortune; but I am still waiting for that day.

My Father built me a large, wooden theatre with the help of my Mother. It had lights and all the gear. I played for hours, if not days, dreaming up plays and musicals. My poor parents had to sit through all my efforts. I think one show included my train set stopping on stage to pick up my paper actors.

Who needs the London Palladium?

The stage lights used to constantly fuse, tripping the entire house. I think Uncle Bertie had to intervene to make everything safe. My Mother had made a real velvet front curtain, which looked exactly like the real thing. I also had some puppets, which were roughly the same size as the stage; I was in seventh heaven.

I just remembered that I also had a circus complete with plastic clowns etc. My parents built a circular ring. More shows for them to watch.

The chimney sweep called twice a year with his rods and set of brushes, they went right up the chimney and out through the chimney pots. Very Mary Poppins! I used to be sent outside so I could tell the chimney sweep when I saw the brushes appear. I suspect this was just to get me out of the way. However, I was happy to fulfil this role as the house tended to get covered in soot.

You may recall Auntie Dorrie's mangle?

My Mother, with my help (?), would take the washing which had already been washed by hand using a washing board and scrubbing brush complete with carbolic soap, round to Number 10. The mangle consisted of two large rubber rollers and a big handle. You placed each piece of washing through the rollers, while turning the handle as hard and quickly as you could manage. The water was collected in a large tin bucket, strategically placed underneath this contraption. I believe most women in those days developed very strong-arm muscles.

Then came the very first Hoover washing machines, which basically were a large container on wheels which you filled with water via a hose pipe attached to the hot water tap. There was an electrically-driven wheel fitted to the inside of the container, which helped turn the clothes. You then had to empty the Hoover by suction, again via the rubber pipe this time into the sink. The pipe often fell out of the sink and soaked the kitchen floor. Everything else still had to be done by hand, but the Hoover washing machine was considered revolutionary at the time.

Croydon Airport closed in 1959. After the war it became both a flying club and a passenger airline with Dakota aircraft, transporting passengers around Europe.

The airport closed in a flurry of controversy with the then Transport Minister's effigy being burnt in the middle of the airfield! I remember going up to the Purley Way playing fields, which were adjacent to the airport, to see the final passenger plane take off. Literally thousands of people went to witness the event. The plane took off and flew three circuits of the airfield dipping its wings before flying off (into the sunset?).

On my way back home from Secondary School, my bus journey took me past the airport, you could almost touch the planes as they came into land.

My other memory of the airport was while I was watching a Saturday afternoon football match taking place on the adjacent playing fields. Suddenly everyone became very aware that the aircraft engine seemed extra loud. A casual glance showed that the plane wasn't going to make the airport runway. We scattered in every direction as the aircraft landed safely in the middle of the pitch. Wow that was close!

Many years earlier my parents gave me a three-wheel tricycle for my birthday. I was totally thrilled and spent many a happy hour on the pavement outside Number 9 pedaling furiously all the way down the hill. I think one day I may have reached 15mph? Years later Mrs Potter told me that my bike had developed a terrible squeak that went on for many years, but I never heard anything. My Mother never allowed me to ride a two-wheeled bike and this is why I still couldn't balance when we had our holidays at Center Parcs!

As a child my health became my Mother's priority. I had a 'dose' of cod liver oil and malt every day until I rebelled at the age of 21! This came in a huge, brown jar in the form of a sticky thick liquid, which smelt and tasted like fish. It was truly revolting but I suspect it may have done some good.

If I developed a cough, then a cotton wool and mustard hot poultice was applied to my chest. When the poultice was cold the trick then was to try and remove it in one go, which didn't always happen. I recall that this treatment was both hot and itchy. Urgh! I preferred the Vicks VapoRub.

I suffered from hay fever when I was a growing lad. Apart from having regular weekly injections, my lovely Mother gave me honeycombs to eat. It must have cost a fortune? Now they were great.

I grew up with a lovely dog called Sally. She was a black and white cocker spaniel. Sally had several litters of puppies, which I remember being born in the cupboard under the sink. Sadly she died, but we kept one of her puppies that later contracted 'hard pad'. The vet came and gave her an injection informing us that the puppy would either survive or die the following day.

Charlie, our cat, cuddled up to our lovely puppy keeping her warm and licking her clean. After several hours, Charlie suddenly left the dog. Our puppy died about an hour later. Strange how animals know. Charlie was great at catching mice.

He cornered them and just stared at them for hours. Often the mouse just keeled over and died.

Another one of Charlie's talents was catching birds. He usually presented each bird in our kitchen normally still alive! However, one day he clearly met his match. He killed a bird which turned out to be the leader of the pack. From that day forward, every time Charlie went outside into our garden the birds set up a huge cacophony of noise. They then dive-bombed him swooping low just above his head. He used to lie prone for what seemed like hours before the birds let him move. I think he learnt his lesson the hard way?

My Father used to clean his nose out using salt water. You could hear him sniffing away in the bathroom. Strange but true.

During the 1950s/60s my Father used to work as a 'dresser' at some of the West End Theatres. I have no idea how that happened but it did. There was a movie and stage star called Ethel Revnell who always asked for my Father when she was in town. I remember having a picture of her addressed to me and signed 'Ethel' with a large kiss; I suspect I didn't know who 'Ethel' was at the time!

I have no idea how my parents met Fred and Dorrie Paris, but they were very friendly with them during the war years. The story goes that when the siren sounded, they used to go under the snooker table at their house. However, they became my godparents. Every year Uncle Fred and Auntie Dorrie used to take me to the Bertram Mills Circus at Olympia in London. Their daughter Pat also came, of course, but I have no idea if we held hands.

I also remember being taken to London to see the Christmas lights and walking around Hamleys toy shop. On one such occasion we were crossing the road and were stopped halfway across on a traffic island, as usual the London traffic was crawling along and suddenly my Mother gasped because in the car immediately beside us were the Queen, the Queen Mother and Princess Margaret. My Mother in her confusion tried to curtsey and got me to bow. All three burst into laughter and waved at us as the car moved off. My Mother naturally dined on this story for some years.

My little family, my Mother, Father and me, visited the Festival of Britain, which took place in 1951 in Battersea. There were plenty of rides, ice cream and a mini dome. This was a very much smaller version of the current O2 Dome. I don't really remember that much about it but my Father recorded the day on his Super 8 ciné camera, so we used to have evenings where the Festival was revisited.

Oh yes and there were fountains and gardens, which still exist.

My Father's Super 8 camera was his pride and joy. As a result he often took movies of his mum when visiting her in Hove. We also had some vintage 1920s/30s silent movies including 'The Flying Scotsman'. We used to watch this film over and over again. The hero was chasing the villain across the roof of the carriages while the heroine sobbed. A sort of very early James Bond!!

There were movies of Grandma Starbuck and Auntie Mabel. Grandma always used to dress for the occasion and posed. I seem to recall that she often wore a hat with some sort of veil? Sadly none of these films have survived the passage of time.

My Primary School(s)

I went to Christchurch Primary School which, at the time, was situated in the centre of Purley. It was some 20+ years later that it moved to its new site where most of the Starbucks attended.

There were three basic things wrong with my school:

First, Miss Try – a very scary headteacher – who according to everyone, including my Mother, was a 'right cow'! I was sick all over my new school shoes in the playground on my very first day because Miss Try shouted at me!

Second, the school was built right over the Bourne River which, although underground, would sometimes flood via the local drainage system. One very wet and cold day I remember being taken out of the classroom over the shoulder of a fireman as the school flooded to such an extent that we all had to be evacuated.

Finally, my parents, bless them, found out that they had sent me to the wrong school!!! In those days, Purley Council was separate from Croydon. Although my Mother would never admit that 9 The Close was actually in South Croydon, I had to move to the Howard of Effingham School in Croydon.

I don't recall a great deal about my new Primary School except:

Mr Wilson, the headteacher, always seemed to have a kind word for everyone.

When I was in Year 3, the teacher, a Mr Francis, left and we had a series of temporary teachers, including a guy called Russell Quay. He brought in his guitar and we sang songs almost all, if not all, day. Later I saw him on 'Top of the Pops' – Russell Quay and the City Rollers (I think!).

Each day everyone had a third of a pint of milk! In the winter the tops used to come off and the frozen milk looked like a candle.

Miss Smee was our Year 5 teacher, complete with brown suede shoes and socks and what always seemed to be the same long brown dress. She was a very prim but fair teacher. We had weekly spelling and maths competitions and depending on the number of correct answers you either moved forward to the front top right desk (you were a young Einstein if you achieved this level). I was much more to the left. When my class left Howard School, a group of us went to say goodbye to Miss Smee and said we all appreciated her help; she cried.

Mr Ives was our Year 6 teacher. This year was better known as the 11+ year. Success in the 11+ exam meant you went to grammar school, failure meant a 'sink' secondary school. Fortunately there was also a middle way called 'central selective' and guess what, that was me! So I ended up at Heath Clark School in Waddon now fortunately defunct and since bulldozed to the ground. Mr Ives was an excellent teacher, especially as I was chosen for the school cricket team! It was Mr Ives who first called me 'Bunter' (he had overheard my friends calling me this). For the rest of my school life no one ever called me Roger; even for the school register I was Bunter.

In those days 'Billy Bunter' was all the rage and did not, as far as I was aware at the time, have any negative connotations. But yes I was plump for my age and I did have 'tree trunk' legs, which allowed me to kick a football further than anybody else.

At Heath Clark School, Bunter morphed into 'Bunner', which just about sums up my 'South London and Proud' school!

I also learnt to play the piano, which had belonged to my grandparents (on my Mother's side). When first installed it was

15

made of lightwood and had brass candlestick holders (really!). However, my Mother got it into her head to have the piano refurbished to a shiny black façade without the candlesticks! Later she would find out from a piano expert that she had effectively significantly decreased the value. Doh!

Although I sort of liked playing the piano I can remember many a row with my parents who, in my view, were forcing me to practice. Usually this involved me giving in eventually, thumping the piano for all it was worth, followed by a relative calm practice session. My tutor was a lovely lady who lived in South Croydon. Her name was Miss Wiseman; she was calm, mostly patient and certainly very wise.

I never considered myself to be very good. In those days it was practicing scales over and over again, a bit of theory plus the Minuet in G. Each year I was entered for the Royal College of Music Exams, which were held in most towns. Looking back at my certificates, I realised that I had attained Grade 8 played in front of audiences at the Annual Prize Giving held at Croydon Town Hall.

I still thought I was rubbish though. I could never sight read or, even better, sit down and play any tune without music. I still envy those with such magical musical skills.

Peter Alliker

When I was about four years old my parents, without my permission, decided that they would like to adopt a child.

We visited a Dr Barnardo's Children's Home, on Pampisford Road, Purley.

Peter Alliker entered our lives. Initially Peter came for weekends only, before joining our family on a full-time basis. I might have been jealous, but I recall enjoying his company. Peter was roughly five years younger than me, so he started at Howard School when I was still in Year 6. Very soon he was found to be nicking stuff from the cloakrooms. However, it must have become a great deal worse as after consultation with the Children's Officer, a frequent visitor to Number 9, Peter gained a place at the Rudolf Steiner Special School in East Grinstead.

Open days were special as soon as you entered. In the school there was an overall feeling of tranquillity. The walls were painted pastel colours, starting with a lighter shade at the top of each wall and gradually going to a darker shade of the same colour at floor level (I have no idea to this day how they managed this). Peter played the violin at open evenings.

Peter was caught removing the lead off the school roof on several occasions, before being finally asked to leave. By this time, my parents were probably rather relieved that they had never formally adopted him. They must have been rather sad that Peter was not the son they had hoped for, but they continued to support him even during his numerous periods in various jails.

Many of you, assuming you have stayed with me, will remember a number of huge lorries Peter used to drive. The Close was his greatest feat of driving skills. We never knew when he would turn up, but if he hadn't visited for a year or so this usually meant he was in prison.

Peter's background was tragic. At Barnardo's, when aged 3-4, he had very nearly been taken back by his mother, only to have his hopes dashed at the last minute. Much later in his life, Peter discovered that he had a twin sister. Apparently, his mother had taken his sister, but not him; this must have been devastating. Unfortunately his sister, who had later moved to America, died before Peter could make contact. Peter enjoyed some happiness in his life, but a great deal of grief.

He always called my parents, Mum and Dad.

Some years ago, during one of his longer spells without making contact, I heard that Peter had died. I went to the funeral, which was paid for by the local council. A handful of his current neighbours attended plus me, the council official and the minister, who would conduct the short service.

The minister asked if anyone would like to say a few words, as otherwise the service would be over in a couple of minutes. As nobody volunteered I said a few impromptu words about his earlier life. Laughter was soon ringing out as his neighbours knew very little of his past, while they happily told me what they knew.

The council officer said that she would arrange for Peter's ashes to be placed near the cemetery lake, which I guess was a big step up from what was a pauper's funeral.

The Oval

Apart from the piano, I enjoyed playing and watching County Cricket. Not that surprising as my Father was into cricket, having played for Bexhill CC. We used to visit the Oval Cricket Ground in Kennington to watch Surrey play.

In those days I suffered from motion sickness. We caught the 109 bus, which started in Purley and went past the Oval. I often had to get off the bus on a regular basis throughout the journey. My poor Father must have been in bits. These were the heady days of Lock, Laker, Surridge and the Bedser twins, when Surrey won the Championship title seven years in a row. Still a record to this day. Later in my teens, we discovered that Allders, then a large independent department store in Croydon, ran an indoor cricket school situated near Surrey Street Market. The cricket nets were organised by the manager of their Sports Department, who turned out to be an ardent Surrey supporter. Lock and Ken Barrington (both regular England players) plus other Surrey county players all used to coach there. I had a great time going once a week for lessons. I vividly remember McIntyre, the Surrey and England wicketkeeper, telling me that if I dragged my right foot again when batting the next week he would put a stake in the ground and tie my right ankle to it. I did drag my foot and, as promised, he tied my leg to a stake. Ever since then I have never dragged my right leg. While I played cricket, before retiring at the age of 24!, I always felt the rope around my ankle when batting.

I was never stumped!

In the 1960s, it was impossible to become a Surrey member as the waiting list was something like 20 years! The manager of Allder's Sports Department however, said it wouldn't be a problem. Within a week I received my free season ticket to the pavilion, plus a Surrey Brown tie which was compulsory to wear. Later I found out that my proposer was Peter May (who was the England and Surrey Captain) and the seconder Ken Barrington, who famously played for England in 82 Test matches. No wonder I received my membership inside a week! Not only could I now sit in the hallowed pavilion for all County and Test matches played at the Oval, I was also now eligible to attend the schoolboy nets, held every year during the Easter holidays.

My first experience one March day was exciting, but I had decided to take my own stumps and ball with me as I wasn't sure what to expect; this was, to say the least, acutely embarrassing. The nets were always taken by a Surrey first team member.

My second visit the same week was not so successful. Also in my nets was an 18-year-old, fast bowler from Charterhouse School and I was first up to bat. This guy ran in from about 40 yards and bowled so fast, I couldn't even see the ball. He hit me all over my body, and I mean all over. I don't think I saw, or played, a ball for him. I can still feel those bruises as I write. I returned home limping and scarcely able to see through my vale of tears.

I thought I would never go to the Oval ever again!

But I did. I have never seen my Father move so fast. He exploded down the phone at some poor guy at the Oval and told him, in no uncertain terms, what he thought of Surrey Cricket Club. In fairness, I think Surrey were horrified this had been allowed to happen. Clearly there is a huge difference physically between a plump 14-year-old (me!) and an 18-year-old lad (Charterhouse as well!).

I was ordered to go straight back up to the Oval the next day (minus my stumps and ball) and report to Peter May, the

England and Surrey Captain. We met in the middle of the Oval, along with my coach from the previous day, where he apologised profusely and I was immediately allowed to bowl in the first team nets – wow!

The next year I played in practice matches, held again at the Oval. This time the fast bowler was on my side. I recall he broke a stump while bowling. I always wondered what happened to him. The good thing was that I never ever encountered anyone in club cricket that bowled that fast!

For some extraordinary reason, my Father took me to see Crystal Palace play when I was around 15. He chose Palace v Millwall!!

We stood on the terraces of what is now the Arthur Waite stand. I think Millwall scored and my Father did his nervous laugh, only to be descended on by a group of Palace fans. I had to get them off him by shouting, "He's my Dad, he doesn't know anything about football!". They then instantly retreated, mumbling he had chosen the right game to come to! No idea what the final score was. My Father never went again, but I was totally hooked, with cricket relegated to second place.

He must have wondered why he ever took me.

More about Palace later, showing my continuing undying devotion of some 60 years and still counting!

Our Relatives

During the war my Father worked for the Norwegian Embassy in London before being called up.

At the time, the German bombing of the London docks had just begun, so the need for firemen was of paramount importance. So, my Father became a fireman one night attending the 'Fire of London' on his first day, not even knowing how to hold a hose. However he must have made an impression at the Embassy, as after the war he received a Christmas hamper for several years from 'a grateful Norwegian family'. We were still on rations at the time, so this hamper was very well received by my little family. We were also sent Christmas decorations, some of which were still around many years later.

Anyway, back to the war!

Unlike many men of that era, my Father was more than happy to talk about his war experiences. The most famous one was dropping his sandwiches into the Thames while struggling with his hose! More interestingly, he was one of a small group of firemen who 'arrested' a German pilot, who had been shot down somewhere over Shirley Hills near Croydon. Apparently, or so his story goes, both sides were initially terrified of each other but soon started chatting away (the German pilot spoke English); they took him for a drink in the local pub before handing him over to the authorities. It's a great story, probably exaggerated over the years!? I know he definitely drove a fire engine with a tender on the back, as years later he always took any corners in a half circle as he still allowed for the non-existent tender!

Anyway back to my relatives. Unlike most families, I didn't have many living relatives.

On my Father's side, there was my grandma known to me as Grandma Starbuck. Her husband had died during the 1930s, long before I came along. She lived with Dorothy, her unmarried daughter, who was always very nice to me when we visited. In later years I found out that she was actually having a passionate affair with the local married bank manager, which went on for some 20-odd years. She was often known as 'Daffy Dorothy' for the obvious reason that she was. Sadly, later in life, she used to ring my Father up at 2am in the morning to ask if she should put the oven on for her Sunday lunch. My Father's other sister was Mabel who married Don Foley, a very quiet guy who chomped on his 'loose dentures' almost the entire time. They and the Starbucks lived in Brighton, well Hove actually, as this was deemed to be the posher side. Mabel had a beach hut on the Hove seafront. She always told me that there was sand at low tide, so I spent many an hour waiting for the sand to appear. It never did!

My Mother was not well liked by the Hove crowd and she didn't like them much either, so we only tended to see them a couple of times each year. My Mother, in her defence, always told the story about the time she first started going out with my Father. She stayed the night with the Hove Starbucks and was charged for a night's stay! Apparently, Grandma Starbuck used to run a Bed and Breakfast.

When visiting Mabel and Don's bungalow, I was always being told off if I opened a door without using the handle – not that I could reach a handle at the time. Apparently, it was just in case I left dirty finger marks. When unwrapping presents, everyone had to hand back the paper for re-use the following year. Although I think I quite enjoyed visiting, I was in total awe of Grandma Starbuck. So much so that I remember her asking my parents, "does he speak?".

Christmas time was the event of the year at Hove. Grandma Starbuck always insisted on cooking the meal right into her 90s.

This cooking event was always accompanied by several sherries, which took place out of sight in her kitchen. By the time dinner was ready she used to unsteadily weave her way from kitchen to dining room, extremely red faced, holding the turkey on a platter.

Grandma would insist on carving the turkey in front of everyone. The older men always used to whisper that if someone was served a larger portion than everyone else they were destined to do very well in her will. Grandma became increasingly deaf as the years went by and would often say, "I can hear what you are saying you know". She clearly couldn't hear everyone, but the message was loud and clear. Afterwards she would cheat at cards but would become quite put out if anyone suggested that she wasn't playing by the rules.

Many years later I became quite friendly with Mabel. It was, after all, her that set up my Father on a blind date with my Mother, and he was engaged to be married at the time!! More about this later …

I used to ring Mabel every Sunday morning at 11am at her nursing home. After my Father died she was the sole survivor and she said sadly there was nothing to live for now. With all her friends and family now dead, Mabel refused to eat and was taken to Brighton Hospital. Later I received a call to say that she was dying. I vividly remember rushing to the car and driving as fast as I could to Brighton. I left the car, illegally parked by the hospital entrance, with something making me run down the corridor. She died seconds before I reached the ward. Much later I collected a few mementos from her nursing home, including a small amount of money, something like £10.55. I declared £10.50 to the solicitors, only to find that one family member was angry that I had kept the 5p!

People can be very strange when it comes to wills.

On my Mother's side, there were even fewer relatives. My grandparents both died when I was very young. I remember them being very kind and loving. My grandfather was first to pass away. At the time we were on one of our many holidays at Bognor Regis. We were having our evening meal when the landlady burst through the door to say that my Mother had to ring an emergency number. In the days before social media and mobiles, the BBC used to announce at 6pm every evening any urgent messages, where contact by phone had failed. My grandfather's impending death clearly fell into this category. My Mother travelled back by trains but I think she was too late. Within six months, my grandma also died in our house of a 'broken heart', which people did in those days.

One of the most talked about occasions was a visit from Alice and John who lived in America. They were on my Mother's side of the family, but what relatives they actually were I am not too sure. They shipped their huge car from the States by boat, so they must have been absolutely minted! The whole Close came out to see this huge American Cadillac trying to edge its way round the rose roundabout. Cadilacs had really only been seen in films. It was talked about for years.

The only other thing I remember from their visit was Alice only wanting half an egg for breakfast, much to my Mother's disgust. Later Alice retired to bed as England was so cold. There was an Aunt Addy née Young, who we visited a few times in her little cottage with uneven floors and ceilings somewhere near Sandwich, Kent. She also died when I was relatively young.

Finally, there was Bertie and Vye Dykes. Bertie was my Mother's older brother. Bertie (although relatives in Canada always said he was called Bert) was a self-made man and worked in accountancy, oil and, rather strangely, selling executive swimming pools!

Vye lost Bertie most of those jobs, usually by insulting whoever was his boss. Vye was a vivacious blond and it was easy to see how Bertie must have fallen for her. Her dress sense and make up made her look immaculate as I recall. However, there was always something a little strange about Vye, apart from my Mother not liking her very much. I think the feeling was mutual.

Later I found out that Vye had undergone electric shock treatment when she was younger, but clearly it hadn't worked. One meal time she put sugar on my peas and when I said I didn't like peas with sugar on top very much, she emptied the sugar shaker all over my dinner! Their house. which was in Waddington Way, South Norwood was both detached and stylish. I loved their garden as Bertie had built a fishpond on two levels with a waterfall between the two. The grass was immaculate and there was croquet lawn in the back garden. However, my most overriding memory was the tiger skin on the floor of their lounge, complete with a bullet hole in it's forehead and open mouth showing all its teeth; hardly PC these days. My parents and I watched the Queen's Coronation in 1952 on Bertie and Vye's black and white TV. Not many people had a TV in those days.

This was the very first BBC outside broadcast, not only showing the ceremony but also their journey down the Mall. To make things a little more interesting, Bertie had purchased some coloured gels, which you put in front of the TV, to make things a little more colourful! We sat watching for the whole day. I recall some of the splendour but suspect this might be helped by the many repeats shown over the years. My Father became so involved that he nearly passed out. Well, I think that is what happened? It was, however, a very memorable and exciting occasion for everyone.

Bertie used to do a few conjuring tricks for me, including the usual disappearing penny. However, his favourite was 'swallowing' a number of cut throat razor blades, and then producing the same blades on a piece of string. Again, this would probably not pass the current Health and Safety brigade. My uncle was very clever with his hands. I vividly remember him building me a fort one Christmas, complete with a working wooden drawbridge plus soldiers and indians! There were loads of clues around the house that Christmas, which finally led me to the fort. Wow it was great and I remember playing with it for many hours. The following year he made a garage, complete with a car showroom with a semi-circle of 'glass'. There was also a car park and petrol pumps reached by a lift, I was in heaven!

Bertie was musical director for a number of local musical societies around the south of England, including the Croydon Stagers. Although I have written a separate chapter on the Stagers, it is worth mentioning his role in my childhood. I would see him from a very early age conducting the pit orchestra for the Stagers' musicals. I remember sitting with him in the orchestra pit during one matinée show. I saw, for the first time, the practical reality behind the showbiz gloss! Any MD has to concentrate for the entire show to be able to pick up on all the musical cues, especially if the actors miss out a few pages of dialogue. Years later, as the juvenile lead, I remember singing a song from 'Flower Drum Song', seeing the panic on Bertie's face; I had started singing the final verse first! Would I go back to the correct verse or just complete the song? Urgh! I also saw the reality of an individual member of the band missing their entrance or, even worse, becoming totally lost. "Bar 55" he would hiss, although I suspect his language may have been slightly tempered by my presence? Looking back, some of his orchestra musicians were probably not that brilliant but generally speaking, the standard was high.

Bertie never praised, or made any comments whatsoever, about my singing (once I had reached the dizzy level of playing leading roles). This was probably because he wanted to remain neutral. I think I wrote a letter to him rather upset that he had never commented on anything that I had achieved. As a result, he suddenly started praising me to the skies, so much so that I had to tell him to stop! When I started to direct musicals, he came to see a few of my efforts, even though by this time he was very ill with cancer. One of my leading ladies later told me that he couldn't stop talking about me.

Bertie joined the army as a cavalry officer and later was assigned to the First Royal Tank Regiment, formed by the British Army in 1916 during World War I. In those far off days the tanks were very slow, often death traps with the German Army picking them off one by one. However, they were very difficult to stop and could easily go straight over the trenches.

I never remember Bertie talking much about his exploits in WWI, but it was either the 50th or the 75th anniversary that he went back to France. They had helped liberate France and Belgium and had often been on the front line. Bertie thought that all those years later, they would be long since forgotten. The French turned out in their droves, with the roads lined with flags and people often five deep. I think there was also an

27

official reception. That was the only time that he choked-up, when showing us the pictures. Sadly, when Heather and I cleared out their house many years later, they were nowhere to be found.

Bertie developed bowel cancer in his later years and I recall going to see him in hospital just after his operation. He gave me a very graphic description, which sent me rushing to the outside corridor. It is, so far, the only time I have come near to fainting. The nurse was yelling at me not to faint, as they had better things to do with their time. Bertie went into hospital a week before he was due to MD a show. I set up a tape recorder at the theatre so that he could hear the show and asked a few of his friends to record messages.

Looking back, I wouldn't say that I was close to Bertie because as a small boy and teenager I was painfully shy. I always gained the impression that my Mother didn't always get on with Bertie that well! Nothing tangible, but it may just have been the older brother and younger sister having to be put firmly in her place.

Except of course she was very much her own woman.

I rest my case.

Heath Clark Central Selective School

I enjoyed the majority of my time at this Heath Clark Central Selective School, having a few close friends throughout my stay and being moderately successful. In order to gain entry into Heath Clark not only did you have to perform reasonably well in the 11+, but you then had to attend an interview hosted by a number of local headteachers.

All the candidates would be asked mental arithmetic questions and I proved to be brilliant at this, as every evening before the interview I was 'grilled' by my Mother on all the times tables up to 12, so much so I can still instantly recall what 9 x 8 are (72!). You also had to read aloud and were then asked questions based on the text.

My Mother's acting ability again meant that I would A* on the day when I came to the reading, but the comprehension element proved to be an absolute disaster.

The reading passage was all about 'loaches'. I hadn't a clue what they were and it felt like an hour before it suddenly dawned on me, they were bloody fish!

My headteacher was a Mr Hislop, the guy who somehow gambled on me even though I didn't know what loaches were! "Be British" and "Chocks away" at the end of each session always punctuated his school assemblies. He was ex-RAF through and through.

There was a Miss Balls (yes that really was her name!), who was my French teacher and also my Form tutor for five years. We all grew to love her. She was tall, thin and always tremendously enthusiastic about everything, whether first thing on a Monday morning or going home time (when we were also enthusiastic!). We once asked what her secret was; she swore it was a lunchtime power nap.

I was always appalling at French, especially the spoken word and used to almost 'die' when it was my turn to read out loud. In the end I think she felt very sorry for me and we came to an agreement that she would only ask me to read once every six months. This helped Miss Balls, the class and myself to relax. When the great day(s) arrived there was complete silence then, as I very hesitantly started to read, the laughter from my classmates started building to a huge crescendo. I was mortified, especially as there were tears of laughter running down Miss Balls' face.

It was then hastily agreed that my reading out loud should only take place once a year on the last day before the summer holidays. Later, however, although I failed my GCSE French I did pass my French oral; if only because Miss Balls had managed to find out the questions just before the oral. I think we all passed?

I only really remember two other teachers. Miss Hills was the headmistress who never smiled and was a real nasty piece of work. She took us for Year 11 maths, didn't know the answers and had to leave the room to look them up. I failed GCSE maths. A few years later, when rehearsing for a Stagers Musical at a local hall, she was on the halls' committee. She still looked extremely stern to put it mildly. I remember her asking me, "Starbuck, could you ask everyone to be quiet". We were an Operatic Society for goodness sake!

Then there was Mr Hayes who taught us English and was always asking the class for the definition of a particular word. Even when looking it up in the Oxford dictionary, he didn't always agree. Later I heard that he had given up teaching and to work for the Oxford Dictionary Company.

Heath Clark was not without its scandals ...

The head girl ran away with the science teacher and was never seen again.

In our final year Ann and Alan who were in my class, who by chance both sat next to each other, became pregnant. I met them both several years later and they fortunately still appeared to be a happily married couple. Come to think of it, both the pregnancy and the couple running away together were probably illegal??

I was still a painfully shy young lad, who spent a great deal of effort trying to avoid any questions posed by my teachers. I think I may have had a year where I might have sworn a great deal and even misbehaved. I was very scared when I clearly tried Mr Hayes' patience too far and he sent me off to be canned by the headteacher. I informed the heads' secretary that I had come to be canned but she said that Mr Hislop was currently teaching and was then out of school for the rest of the day, even though I could quite clearly hear his voice in the study. I think I may have got away with that!

The annual speech days were truly appalling. The guest speakers were clearly never chosen for their presentation skills. The choir was always led by Miss Wilkinson, the music teacher, and they always performed at the commencement of the evening; they were not always very good.

I vividly recall our lovely headteacher commenting at the end of one awful performance, that the best thing he could say about the choir was that they had now stopped! A truly dreadful thing to say even though it was true! My Mother was shaking with silent laughter while Miss Wilkinson sobbed on stage.

There was also the annual play, also usually directed by poor Miss Wilkinson. One year it was so bad that the performance was barracked by us kids plus, I would like to think, by a few parents. There was a specially-convened assembly the following morning, where Mr Hislop walked up and down the rows of students with his cane shouting, "This just wasn't British!".

I think at one point the whole school might have thought we were all going to be canned. However, after about 10 minutes of shouting at everyone, he suddenly burst out laughing and dismissed us all with his usual, "chocks away lads".

Miss Wilkinson remained sobbing her heart out, poor woman.

Mr Owen (yes, he was Welsh) was the PE Teacher. I almost permanently had a sick note, as I hated things all PE.

The school was situated right next to Duppas Hill Recreation Ground, with a steep hill leading up from the school playing fields to a Pavilion at the top. Beyond this there was a series of football and cricket pitches. Cross country meant running up this hill and around the various football pitches, which were out of sight of the school. As Mr Owen never bothered to either walk or run up the initial hill, it was very easy for my group to hide behind the Pavilion situated at the top of the hill and run down fresh as a daisy, coming nicely in the middle of class. He never let on that he knew.

The other exciting yearly event was the sports day, which always took place in June/July. In those days the summer appeared to me to be permanently sunny. I soon realised that if I ran very slowly in the 100 yard trials, then I would have a free day to soak up the sun. One year nobody seemed to want to run in this marathon race, so the whole trial was conducted at a snail's pace, much to the amusement of Miss Balls and, to be fair, Mr Owen. My poor parents used to turn up every year to 'support' me, but all they ever did was eat ice cream with me. I don't think they ever saw me race? 'Bunner' you lazy sod!

I have no idea how the situation arose but, out of the blue, Heath Clark spawned a Debating Society.

For some totally weird reason I volunteered, only to find it was to be an inter-school competition. Yes, I was still reasonably shy but I guess I was just 'commencing' the very long road to becoming a normal human being. Miss Balls was suitably astounded and came along to the first after-school debate. I was amazed too that I had even volunteered! We won and went through to the next round with me just loving it, including all the attention.

When the next debate came around, I immediately spotted most of my teachers sitting in a line along the first row. We lost, but after my debating skills were exposed I suddenly had to answer nearly every single question thrown at me by my teachers. There is always a downside.

Although I regularly played cricket for my school I rarely, if ever, made the football squad. However, for some reason I was selected to play centre half for the school, although I had never played at this position before or since. This was the annual match between the staff and the first team and took place on a very muddy pitch in front of the whole school.

Mr Hislop was playing centre forward, so I was automatically going to mark him …

He was also the referee!

Before kick-off I was informed, in no uncertain terms by the headteacher, that if I fouled him I would immediately be sent off. It was just too much of a temptation!! Within the first 10 minutes he came running at me with the ball at his feet, and then bang he was face down sliding along the muddy pitch. I was, of course, sent off to thunderous applause from the entire school and I suspect a few teachers. I was the school hero, well for the next 24 hours or so.

I didn't realise it at the time, but I clearly had been set up. Looking back now, he must have known that the temptation would be too much for me, or any other pupil for that matter. He was a great sport, a very unusual character, even if he was not a very effective headteacher.

I am now going to let you into a small secret!

Travelling to school, I used to catch the bus to South Croydon and then walk up the hill to my school which was situated in the middle of a rundown council estate. When walking up the hill every day, I used to meet a number of characters coming the opposite way. This included a gentleman in an immaculate suit, bowler hat and umbrella who used to really march down the hill. He told off anyone who was, for example, daring to ride their bikes on the pavement.

We always said, "Good morning" to each other while I imagined he was, at the very least, the Mayor of Croydon. One particular day, he stopped and handed me a present before moving off saying this was his final day before he retired. He looked and sounded so sad.

No that wasn't the secret!

33

One day as I walked up the hill towards my school, I was joined by a young lady called Sue. We held hands and walked up the hill together. I was in seventh heaven, if maybe a little confused, as she was in Year 11 compared to my Year 9 status. After a few weeks of holding hands, Miss Balls (it had to be Miss Balls!), met us at the school gates and suggested to Sue that she really was baby snatching. Sue threw her arms around me and kissed me (I would like to say passionately, but I don't think it was). She disappeared and I never saw her again. Happy times!

I left Heath Clark after just one year in what was then their brand new sixth form. I spent part of that year retaking a couple of O levels (GCSEs) including maths.

The excellent maths teacher, Mr Simons, who was until Year 11 my teacher prior to the infamous Miss Hills. Mr Simons was livid with me for failing maths, which under his guidance I would probably have passed with flying colours.

His solution was a brutal one. I was forced to attend his A* Year 11 class. He gave me a month to bring myself up to speed before throwing every maths problem he could muster at me in front of his Year 11 class. I survived through a mixture of fear and self-preservation. I passed my maths GCSE exam just three months after joining his class. It just shows what a great teacher can do.

As far as 'A' levels were concerned I particularly liked English literature, until I found out the main piece to be studied was T S Eliot's The Waste Land. As the title suggests, there is unremitting gloom and not a laugh in sight. Why wouldn't the choice include 'Cats' by T S Eliot? I might have then gone on to be a Professor of something or an actor?

I parted ways with Heath Clark only to return for a reunion a few years later. My only other 'brush' with the school was to attend its closing down. It was rather a sad occasion and interesting that nearly every teacher at the school during my time also attended.

I guess I must have been at Heath Clark at the best time?

Childhood Holidays

Our holidays were mainly spent in sunny (occasionally) Bognor Regis in West Sussex.

The landlady was a Mrs Fenner, although we stayed just around the corner at Mrs Rough's house, who just provided somewhere to sleep. There was a huge room, well it was probably quite small but it was large in my young eyes, with a jug and bowl for washing. No running water or showers! We had all our meals at Mrs Fenner's, around a large table, which sat 12 guests.

I insisted that we return every year for about 10 years, as I thought Bognor Regis was wonderful. I was allowed to stay up to see the Bognor lights once a year. I think they consisted of just one string of lights!? The highlight was having a lovely milky Horlicks before bedtime.

Every year, Uncle Fred (my godfather) and his wife Dorrie plus their daughter Pat, came with us. Pat later married Alan Yardley of swimming pool fame. There are incriminating pictures of me holding hands with Pat on Bognor seafront, when I was about six years old. Pat is older than me, so perhaps she held my hand? The beach was sandy then, but if you dug down a few inches, the stench of oil hit you. Apparently, a tanker had discharged its oil cargo just a few years prior to me digging sandcastles.

When it rained, we used to build a shelter made from deckchairs. My Father, much to my Mother's annoyance, always used to say, "this was the clearing up shower!". Usually

35

the cue for the rain to suddenly come down in 'stair rods'. We ran for it when that happened.

One year there was a newly-married couple also staying at Mrs Fenner's. They asked if they could take me out for the day. We visited Chichester Cathedral and had a very nice Fish and Chips meal. I have no idea why they took me out, maybe to decide whether to have children of their own, in which case they probably remained childless. Chichester Cathedral seemed perhaps an odd choice, but I remember being impressed and having a very enjoyable day out in their company.

One year, I guess in sheer desperation, my parents took me for a day out to the Isle of Wight. From then on this was the only place to go for summer holidays!

Just one anecdote about Mrs Fenner, who brought up eight sons but would never allow them to play with toy guns. We later read in the newspaper that her eldest boy had been arrested during an unsuccessful bank raid, complete with guns.

I must have been around 16 when we all went by train to Switzerland. Looking back, this was a very progressive thing to do, as it was some years before package holidays. I recall waking up in the morning to witness deep blue lakes and snow, an awe-inspiring sight. We stayed in a place called Weggis on Lake Lucerne. The scenery was breathtaking. I remember going up in one of those very fast lifts, which took us up to the top of a mountain in about one minute flat! Unfortunately you then had to walk across a gangway, which had open slats enabling you to see a 6,000-foot drop. I just froze and nothing my parents could do would make me move. Finally, a teenage girl managed to help me inch my way across.

Many decades later I was at a neighbour's party while living at Brancaster Lane, Purley when I noticed this lady eyeing me up during the early part of the evening. Finally, she came across to me and said, "Hello Roger" which I found very embarrassing as I had no clue as to who she was. Weirdly, it turned out to be the young, teenage girl who had helped me across that bridge in Switzerland all those years ago. She was now living two doors down from us with her children.

It's a small world.

Croydon Corporation

My first job was with Croydon Corporation (now known as the London Borough of Croydon) in their Teachers Salaries Department. The offices in Katharine Street, Croydon were divided up into very small departments. Mine just had four people including myself.

I think I went for the job purely to find out what my former teachers actually earned. I was, in theory, on some sort of fast-track scheme where you moved from department to department. Except nobody ever moved.

My immediate boss was a Mr Borley and within 10 minutes of me arriving I was asked to go to the next-door office to collect a file. As I opened the door of the next office I was met by a couple in a passionate embrace, they were so preoccupied that they didn't even hear me or become aware of my presence. I coughed, they saw me, handed over the required file and then went back to their embrace!

I came back to my new office and handed the file to Mr Borley and sat down at my new desk. Had heaven finally arrived, was office life a den of iniquity? These thoughts flashed through my mind and it was only 9.15am on a Monday morning! Suddenly our office door flew open and in walked the girl from the passionate embrace. She came straight across to me and apologised. Mr Borley and his sidekick Mr Shepherd (a strange embittered man) could not contain their laughter.

Over the next year or so that I was still being paid by the Council, Pauline and I became firm friends. One of my duties was to take files across to the Accounts Department, which at the time was situated in Barclay Road right next to where the now famous Fairfields Halls was being built. By this time, I was well into all things theatrical, so the building of the Halls was exciting to say the least. Around six weeks later, I became friendly enough with some of the workmen on the project to persuade them to allow me onto the stage of the already-built Ashcroft Theatre. I like to think that I was the very first person to stand on this stage. I can still remember my excitement and emotions to this day. I would, during my 20s and 30s, go on to dance (?), sing and play principal parts on this very stage, not to mention direct many musicals.

But that is another story!

There was another young guy in my department and we both took every opportunity to sneak off somewhere more interesting. We used to discuss life in general. He was already in an unhappy marriage. One day he arrived in the office battered and bruised and in a very emotional state. Mr Borley took him back home. Later that day my boss returned to the office and reported that the less I knew the better, but their entire flat had been trashed.

Sadly, I can't remember his name, but his heartbroken face said it all. His image did not leave me for many years. Did I perhaps witness my first example of husband beating?

I never saw my friend again.

Anyway, by that time I had enough of Croydon Council so I left to become a vital cog of the Midland Bank. In reality, I probably contributed to its subsequent demise – being taken over much later by HSBC way after I had left.

The Midland Bank

After my initial training, my first branch was on the Old Kent Road. I was 18 years of age. The branch looked as though it was something out of a Dickensian novel.

There were high, sloping desks that stretch the whole length of the branch with stools that had no backs for staff to sit on. Apart from that, the journey from Purley was horrendous.

I have just one stand out memory, which featured the Bank vaults. More accurately the lift that took the money up to the floor of the Bank. The lift was operated by hand, so you had to turn a large handle until the money had risen from the vaults. The lift had no walls and was, therefore, just an open platform. There were just two problems to overcome: First, the money in notes and coins had to be loaded onto a trolley then pulled by hand onto the lift; money in that quantity is really heavy. Second, the lift handle was not only stiff to turn but also the weight of the money made turning it even more difficult.

This was my first task every morning, which in those far off days included Saturday mornings. One day the almost inevitable happened. I failed to put the trolley brake on as I sweated and heaved to turn the wheel. Suddenly the trolley filled to the brim with money crashed off the open lift and fell, some seven-foot to the floor of the vaults. I could hear the staff laughing as I tried to pick up the money, which was by now all over the floor. I think I might not have been the first?

Back in the 1960s staff had to travel to any branch the Bank felt was necessary. After a few short months my Mother was on the phone to the Head Office. This resulted in a move back, you have guessed it, to CROYDON! My branch was situated at the end of Surrey Street Market so many of our customers were market holders who only dealt in cash. They were great at bringing us fruit and vegetables; well actually it was for the very pretty cashiers, who in turn gave us part of their spoils.

Mr Bailey was the Bank manager. I do remember him receiving a death threat and getting us all together to inform us that we had to watch our backs. What we were quite meant to do I am unsure, but I remember watching my back on my way home to Purley!!

We sometimes had parties outside banking hours usually when Mr Bailey had reached some sort of target. After about an hour of formal drinks he used to leave, handing the Bank keys to anyone who didn't look totally worse for wear. I was often trusted with these keys! The parties then often became wild affairs. In fact, there were a few actual affairs if I remember correctly.

Strangely at precisely 9pm, the party had to stop, by decree of Mr Bailey. If I had the Bank keys, then I had to collect everyone up, which often included the office floor not to mention the stationary cupboard, and then throw them out onto the street taking great care not to leave any member of staff behind. My final task was to put the Bank alarm on and double lock the Bank front doors. I then used to watch my back!

At one such party, I was taken by a senior member of the management team to the basement and was shown the electrical on/off switch, which served the entire branch building. I was informed that if I was ever to gain promotion, I had to flick this switch to the off position as soon as the lift buzzer sounded. Wanting to be promoted, I did exactly as I was told!

Next day my apprehension grew as one by one the girls slowly discovered my role in last night's proceedings. I don't think they could quite believe that this still relatively shy new boy was capable of such a thing! In those days it was considered just good fun and in reality, no one ever got hurt or suffered from flashbacks. It was after all the swinging 60s!

Oh yes, and I did get promoted!

I have fond memories of Linda and Doreen who did so much to bring me out of my shell. They were kind, considerate, helped when I made mistakes and gave me, without fail, a kiss every morning.

Utter bliss for an 18-year-old.

I also met Alan Parkyn, who trained me in many of the Bank's procedures. More about him later.

Sadly, after a couple of years of comparative bliss, I was transferred to the High Holborn Branch in London. This was a very large branch with around 50 staff where the main customer was the Prudential Insurance Company (their Head Office was just up the road).

It beggars belief, but Prudential staff were paid by cheque each month so on pay day there were hoards of people queuing out of the doors to pay in their cheques to receive cash in exchange. This was known as "Pru Day."

Every branch had to make absolutely certain that after the closing time (3pm) every single balance was correct to the very last one old pence, without this happening no one was allowed home. The tension each day was often high as no one could ever make plans to go out in the evening. Strangely, the staff that had to make things balance were the 'waste' team, which in such a large branch was a team of six including myself.

At Croydon if the balance was incorrect then everyone used to come and help. At High Holborn no one did. They just moaned and groaned as time passed. The chief clerk was a Mr Gearey, a fierce man with absolutely no humour, who treated everyone like a piece of dirt. One cold, snowy morning everyone was late arriving as Southern Rail had all but given up. I remember him standing at the door of the Bank shouting, "You're late!" as each person arrived. After leaving the Bank there was once again a similar snowy morning but one of the staff hit him and apparently Mr Gearey never did it again. Not sure what happened to the guy though?

Two good things happened during my London employment at the Bank. I met my first proper girlfriend plus Alan Parkyn, who I first met in Croydon, suddenly turned up to work at the High Holborn branch.

The turning point for me came one afternoon when I was requested by the chief clerk to help with the registers. I hardly knew what they were but on receiving no instructions I did the best I could. The result was a complete and utter disaster.

I was summoned by the Bank manager, who rarely spoke to anyone and asked what the hell I had been doing. Well that was the gist of it anyway.

I blurted out that I had never received any training whatsoever.

He went crimson and dismissed me from his palatial office asking me to send in the chief clerk, Mr Gearey. You could hear the shouting all over the bank as he slowly took Gearey apart. The whole branch went deathly quiet.

I fled the branch and didn't know whether to turn up the following day, so like a good boy I stayed at home with my parents! Wimp that I was! My Bank manager called later that same day and asked me to come and see him. It seemed a very long journey into London as I was fairly certain, for some reason, that I would be fired. In fact, he apologised profusely and even asked if I would like to stay on!

By this time, I had enough. I was off to the Legal and General Assurance Society in Kingswood, Surrey. I think the suggestion came from Pat Yardley, who at the time worked for L&G in, you have guessed it, CROYDON!

I stayed at L&G for exactly 35 years!

The Legal and General
Assurance Society Ltd

I was at Legal and General (or L&G) for 35 years – unbelievable!

I just plan to pick out some of the highlights, funny moments and even a few miserable years. Life at L&G gave me a huge lift to my self esteem and confidence, leading to some exciting and challenging roles. It also gave me my first opportunity to direct shows.

I started working at Kingswood in the winter of 1963. There were 6 foot snow drifts everywhere. The electric train from Purley to Kingswood needed one of the last remaining steam engines to help push it up the steep incline between Chipstead and Kingswood stations.

I think I must have had an interview of sorts, but the main question was, "when can you start!".

Their recruitment process was almost non-existent and so were internal communications. Clearly my arrival in Pension Claims was unexpected to say the least. Later, my section leader and his deputy admitted that they had gone outside and jumped up and down with excitement. Not because it was me but, apparently, they had been requesting more staff for over a year and I was their first; and as it turned out their sole success. Needless to say, it was a very busy team.

The main change of style was that everyone called each other by their first name but we still had to keep our suit jackets on at all times. All women employees had to wear a plastic-looking overall, which apparently had been designed by the famous fashion designer, Norman Hartnell, clearly on a very bad day! If a girl married, then they had to leave L&G.

One of my early section leaders was called Mike Fowler; he constantly sucked pastels so his tongue and lips were always bright red. He enjoyed his cricket and I was soon asked to join the L&G cricket team. On my arrival for my first match I was met by the captain who immediately warned me never to speak to the pretty girl standing to one side of the rest of the players and supporters. This poor girl was the wife of Mike Fowler. In the past there had, apparently, been fights between Mike and whoever had the misfortune to speak to Mrs Fowler. I did what I was told and never spoke to her; a shame really as she always looked so lonely.

I promised you some funny moments that happened during my 35 years and Mike features in my first anecdote. In each wing of the office there were about 100 staff and, by this time, Mike was the man in charge of my wing. To overcome being forbidden to remove jackets, the senior management team resorted to wearing lightweight white jackets during one very hot summer. One day Mr Standring, our Senior Director, came down the corridor towards us. You could hear him coming for miles as he wore steel-capped heels that made a racket on the wooden floor. Mike said under his breath, "Look out, here comes the ice cream man". Later in the afternoon we again heard Bobby Standring clip-clopping down the corridor towards us, perhaps a little slower than normal, he had bought everyone an ice cream! Bless him, although my more vivid recollection was Mike's red face which for once matched his red lips.

Bobby Standring was clever but very eccentric. He once painted his stairs at home from top to bottom one evening. Bobby and his wife had to sleep downstairs that night while the paint dried.

Procedure was that pension claims over a certain amount had to be signed off by Bobby. He took personal exception to signing away L&G's funds, so would write to each customer explaining other investment options. He had a habit of placing all such files in his hat stand situated behind his office door; sometimes for weeks on end. He always went to lunch at exactly the same time each day, so it was my job (why was it always me?) to search through his stand for any missing files. This method worked extremely well, except one day he came back from his lunch early with me still stuck behind his door! I decided to stay where I was in the hope that he would shortly leave his office. However, this plan failed when Bobby announced, "Starbuck, you can come out from behind my door!". He was chuckling away to himself, but Bobby never kept his files in the hat stand ever again!

I have already mentioned that the recruitment policy was not that great. Apart from recruiting me, the Personnel Department once employed a typist without noticing she only had one arm.

Then there was 'Harry the Horse'. Sadly Harry thought he was a horse and used to 'gallop' up and down the corridors. He was employed for several years, mainly because we became used to his cantering to work every day. He was also fed oat biscuits by his mates. However, his demise came when, one year, he requested time off to run in the Epsom Derby; sadly he was fired.

Then Alan Parkyn turned up, the guy who had trained me at Midland Bank. Apparently, he was working in a section just around the corner from me! We remained friends for many years, having lunch together and sometimes meeting socially. I do have a very guilty conscience as, in all honesty, I dropped our dinner time lunches once I became involved with the Pension Review Team (which later formed such a chaotic part of my life) as I was just too busy to have lunch. But, the longer I left not seeing him, the worse it became, more of an embarrassment really. Later I heard that Alan had left L&G after a failed eye operation and no one knew where he had moved to? I am so sorry Alan.

Perhaps before I write further, I ought to explain this huge office complex situated in the middle of the Surrey countryside. The story goes that during World War II L&G moved key staff out of London to a former girls' school, St Monica's, which formed part of the Kingswood Estate. Apparently after the war the girls never returned and the school plus the surrounding land was purchased by L&G. It was a huge area surrounded on three sides by farms. On the fourth side, you either arrived by train or drove up to the gates passing through the equivalent of £6 million plus houses. Needless to say the residents never liked us, especially when the staff increased from around 50 to somewhere in the region of 4,000 in the 1990s. In the 1950s, large offices were built in the grounds with the school becoming a restaurant, where you could buy lunch for just 5p. Oh, I nearly forgot, there was also an outdoor swimming pool, tennis courts and cricket and football pitches. Sometimes deer from the surrounding countryside came to graze or to watch us work.

Time for another anecdote.

In the early 1960s, huge computers were installed at what must have been enormous expense.

They were valve driven, placed on top of the huge computer 'boxes'. That first Christmas we took it in turns to enter this brand new computer complex, which was roughly 200 yards long, to hear 'Jingle Bells' played via the computer valves! Very nice it was too, as each lit up as well!

On returning to work in the New Year, it became very apparent that our new computers were not functioning as they should. Well actually most of the valves didn't work at all, so there was no computer system. As a result, we were never allowed to visit the computer suite ever again. Actually, I don't think we were ever meant to be there in the first place! It must have cost a small fortune to replace everything.

I already mentioned the nylon-style overalls the girls had to wear ... One very warm summer these overalls became unbearably hot, so many resorted to not wearing very much underneath. The overalls were quickly scrapped when it was realised that in a certain light, you could see straight through them! We could now, at long last, also take our jackets off!

Over my first decade, I went from humble clerk through to deputy then to section leader in charge of around 30 staff. Shortly before I left in the 'swinging' 1990s, every member of staff was allowed to see their own personnel file (after some heavy redaction had taken place in Personnel!). A certain senior director had added this comment in my 1960s file, "Roger Starbuck looks like a man on a mission and is clearly one to watch!". This was a great comment, but I had never even spoken to him! Lovely man though!

One of my managers who stood out for all the wrong reasons was a certain, well, let's call him Jim. A very good local cricketer who just loved a drink or two plus many more. Jim always drank eight pints of draught Guinness every lunchtime. I know this for a fact, as I was with him on one occasion! Jim had one quite amazing talent, he never showed that he was worse for wear, speaking normally and able to walk in a straight line. However, I soon discovered that after lunch he was 'brain dead'. I'm afraid I took full advantage by making certain that every decision I required was always presented to him in the afternoons. It was a great way to do business.

Later Jim would combine three whole sections, bringing over 60 staff under my control. Now this was around the time my first wife had just left me, so I wasn't really in quite the right frame of mind. Perhaps he thought that he was doing the right thing by taking my mind off personal matters, or more likely he had finally noticed my afternoon decision strategy?

Around this time, quite out of the blue, a member of the L&G Drama Group popped in to see me. I was asked if I would like to direct their next play. It was well known that I was into am-dram, with a few staff members having had the misfortune to attend my performances. I think I may have been playing the third chorus member in the back line at the time. As it subsequently turned out, this was the start of something quite significant in my life.

1.   I gained another promotion to a senior management role.

2.   Life as an amateur director of plays and musicals was about to take off.

But more about both later.

Hu Mann was known as the 'Squire of Kingswood' as he was, in effect, in charge of some 4,000 staff; in other words the entire building! One of his more onerous duties was to attend the L & G Drama Group shows, which usually consisted of a Christmas panto plus a play in the Spring. Poor guy, although in my particular case it clearly worked in my favour!

47

I came back from holiday one August, only to find out from my staff (this was the combined three sections previously mentioned) that Hu Mann urgently wanted to talk to me. A cold sweat descended as I immediately thought of all the cover ups I had achieved over the years, not to mention my decision-making via the lovely Jim.

"Starbuck, in my office now!" thundered Hu from 50 yards away. God, I thought this is going to be bad and it's only 9.30 on a Monday morning. However, Hu was all smiles and immediately informed me that in my absence he had made me Training Manager for the whole of Kingswood House. I hadn't seen that one coming. I may have stammered "why me", immediately being informed that if I was stupid enough to direct L&G staff in panto, most of whom had little or no talent, then I was the perfect choice! Hu always appeared laid back and carefree, but months later I found out that many of the staff who had taken part in my pantos had been 'grilled' by him asking if I was a suitable choice. Not quite as laid back as he might have appeared then.

Anyway, I had a great few years developing and running courses and workshops on every conceivable subject. My drama background helped me presentation wise. Clearly, I had at last overcome my shyness and my nerves. I had a clean slate as this was a brand-new position, so within reason I was allowed to develop and run sessions without interference.

Great fun, but hard work.

After several years, which included teaming up with external consultants, L&G decided to run their very first Graduate Recruitment Scheme. All graduates were invited to come for the entire day. The day consisted of formal interviews (think 'The Apprentice'), psychometric testing by external consultants and a whole lot more. An average day now, but in the 1980s, fairly revolutionary.

The set up was impressive, but often in reality revolved around just one thing, whether or not L&G reception staff thought that the candidates were any good. If they didn't like a particular graduate who might have mentioned for example that he (she) had never heard of L&G and wouldn't be staying long

– we just didn't take them. Surprising what people say while waiting in Reception!

As you might have gathered, I was involved in this process, which looking back, was my first brush with the Personnel process. Much later I became part of the Personnel functions.

But as you have probably guessed, that is another story!

I also directed videos at L&G's offices in Milton Keynes. Believe it or not they had a fully-functional TV studio, complete with an editing suite. I ran riot.

Direct Selling was taking off in a big way in the 1980s. L&G had a brand-new Direct Sales Force, who were eligible for their own car! They were paid on a commission-only basis and were often sacked after a few months if they hadn't met their targets. I think one guy drove his car over a cliff after being fired (after getting out first!). Another drove his car to somewhere remote in Scotland and L&G had to guess where he might have left it!

The reason for mentioning our Direct Sales Force was that somehow or other, I was asked to play the part of a customer in their own home being interviewed by the L&G top salesperson. It was to be entirely unscripted with the sales guy's only objective being to sell me a Life Policy. For example, the salesman might say to me, "what nice wallpaper", I would reply that I always hated it.

It was great to do and once again, my 'acting ability' was put to the test. However, the video had unfortunate repercussions for me. Apparently, the video was to be part of the Induction Programme for new salespeople. Every time I went to lunch after the film was released, I had a whole series of would-be salesmen coming up to me trying to sell insurance while I attempted to eat my dinner. This went on for several years, until I finally resorted to producing a laminated message saying something like 'I am an actor – nothing was real!' which I placed next to my dinner plate; but a couple of guys still wouldn't take no for an answer. They all seemed very disappointed.

Then came probably the biggest mistake of my L&G career. I decided that I would really like the Training and Communications vacancy in the Head Office at Temple Court,

London. Although I successfully negotiated the interview process, which also included external applicants, it proved to be a very bad move.

Temple Court was a less than imposing 1960s build. It had actually been moved back from its original position by the road to allow for the ruins of the Temple of Mithras to be displayed. This was the only good or interesting thing about my two-year stay. It was occupied by high-ranking managers who were mostly totally removed from reality, didn't have a clue what was going on but, to make matters even worse, thought they did!

The more interesting aspect revolved around floors 11 and 12.

Floor 11 contained all the directors' offices, but oddly did not have their names on each door. You had to guess, or find one of the very few who knew, which I later found out was the caretaker. The reason given was something to do with the IRA planting a bomb, but I doubt whether they would have worried who was in each office?

Floor 12 housed the Board Room with its very imposing long polished table and leather chairs. This was where the 'City Royalty' were wined and dined at lunchtimes. The thing to do was to blag an invite. The 'Maître De' (yes, we had one!) used to glide around the room with a bottle of wine in each hand. One was for the guests, the other for us staff, which was usually a 1932 Chablis.

Initially I was responsible for writing Operating Instructions, which later might be read by most L&G staff. I was obviously hopeless at this task and frankly hadn't much interest as I knew that most managers and staff didn't read them anyway. My first draft was never given a second glance. One day, one of the senior managers rewrote my entire draft before leaving it on my desk.

Simple I thought, I would give his version to my typist (yes, I had one) asking her to replicate this draft word by word. I then placed it on his desk and went home for the day. The next day he informed me that once again my draft was total rubbish. "But it was your draft", I quietly mentioned. He never spoke to me again!

50

I previously referred to the mysterious 11th floor, for reasons I cannot recall, I had to take a file to one of the directors, so I opened an office door at random. I had quite by chance struck gold as it turned out to be the Chairman of L&G at that time! Now, his daughter Kate had been in a number of my shows. See how drama and work can combine! We had tea together, which included cucumber sandwiches. He was so pleased to see someone he knew and was clearly quite lonely.

I think I returned to my desk, still with the file, about an hour later. I mentioned in passing that I had just had afternoon tea with the chairman. I was aware of a sudden stillness as everyone stopped talking. It was strange as at Temple Court, staff and managers used to almost bow down at directors' feet, but the same directors would visit Kingswood where staff would quite happily chat to them.

It really was a weird place.

Following on from my 'tea party', I received a call a few weeks later from his secretary, asking if I would give her boss some guidance on presentation skills as he had the Societies AGM coming up. I remember going to the dress rehearsal and happily giving him a few pointers. The next day the icy atmosphere in the office from my managers was rather noticeable.

This was the time I spent many weeks away from home running management courses at Nene College in Northampton. It was there that my first allergy surfaced; alcohol!

The only other good thing about the location of Temple Court was its vicinity to Theatreland. So, I became a 'matinée idol' for many of the famous musical shows of the time.

I soon worked out the best way to sit in the most expensive seats. Always go for the cheapest seats in the house and, if the matinée was not full you often got moved to the expensive seats. I remember in particular seeing the musical Chess from the third row of the front stalls, having paid just £15 for the back of the upper circle – yesss!

Then suddenly I was facing redundancy. Due to a radical reorganisation of the entire company structure, training was passed to each individual department.

My role disappeared overnight.

There was the possibility that L&G would give me a lavish redundancy package, but that apparently was far too expensive. Yes, I could have joined Learning Performance, but the company was still in its infancy so this would have been a very high risk.

So, my name and limited CV was passed around the Kingswood Managers.

I was 'saved' by one of my earlier section leaders, who at the time of my first marriage had given me a salary increase to £1,000 per annum (yes really!), so I could have a mortgage of £4,000 to buy my first property. In those days you could borrow four times your salary. Believe it or not when you were about to take out a mortgage, a senior manager from London used to come down and try to talk you out of the mortgage, marriage and responsibilities.

I came back to Kingswood, to a brave new world.

The old Kingswood House had been demolished and replaced by a brand spanking new building comprising all the latest gadgets. Some say that it was beautiful while others thought the opposite.

Its worst feature was the external sun blinds which were meant to come down when the sun came out, but of course mainly remained up in order to achieve maximum light into this mainly glass building. In reality, the blinds spent most of their time going up and down as most days were not cloudless blue skies. Even worse, on really stormy days, the blinds would crash against the glass!

A seismic change had taken place in the way everyone worked. There were no more typists! Everyone had their own IBM computer linked to various main systems, plus there was email! Almost before emails were invented.

Suddenly you were expected to type and understand a particular computer system: Arrgh!

However, things were due to take off for me in a very big way, but first some other great benefits of working for L&G. I have already mentioned the 5p lunches. These were later replaced by luncheon vouchers. We soon learnt to save them up, so they could be used to purchase the weekly shopping so packed lunches became the norm.

In this mainly fabulous new building there was not only a restaurant but a bar, which was open at lunchtime (it closed after a short time as this facility was abused by a minority of staff, including my friend Jim!).

There was also a very good coffee Lounge, which proved very popular with all staff.

Oh, and an outdoor swimming pool and gym.

At some point during my 35 years' employment flexitime came into being. No more 9–5. You could arrive as early as 8am and leave as late as 6pm. The other option was to leave at 4pm. You had to electronically sign in and out, but if you accrued more hours over and above the 35-hour working week, you could take time off in lieu. By achieving this you were entitled to a maximum of 12 extra days holiday per year. It also meant that I could leave early for work in the mornings, but easily be home to read bedtime stories, not to mention bath time!

This was a brilliant perk and was well ahead of its time.

I also became part of Personnel for a brief spell. I am not really sure how, but remember having to make a large number of staff redundant as part of my duties. I was always told that if someone bursts into tears and was really upset when you gave them the sad news, they strangely would be fine. Conversely if they laughed and joked and said things like, ''what a relief'', then you would be in for trouble. Within the hour they would be back swearing and cursing and threatening to hit you.

Sadly, it was nearly always true. Not the happiest of times.

Then it all happened!

I was told very quietly in the corridor that I had to go and see someone urgently, to tell nobody I was going and say nothing when I got back! It was the beginning of the Pension Review Unit, which was being set up in great secrecy. I was going to be the new Training and Recruitment Manager.

In the 1990s, there was a huge scandal in all the National papers, as basically most Insurance Companies had mis-sold their pension schemes, by promising far better returns than was realistically possible to unsuspecting members of the public.

There were just three of us, but this would grow to some 250 staff and countless more temps all within the next nine months.

The L&G directors didn't want anyone to know that the society had in fact mis-sold in a very big way.

I had the most extraordinary remit, with my pension knowledge I had total freedom to go to all Pension departments and pick out those who had the experience necessary to tackle this huge problem. They were given just one weeks' notice before arriving in the new Unit.

This actually meant that I was 'cherry picking' the best staff to the detriment of existing sections, not to mention their managers who were often incandescent with rage. However, I was informed by the directors, who were swarming around looking extremely worried, that if a manager refused to release any staff member I should refer them straight to the directors. I don't think any manager had the courage to pick up the phone.

However, there were only a limited number of experienced staff. Clearly recruitment from other external sources was required, and quickly. I think every recruitment agency around, including Croydon, was set the task of sending me applicants. My desk became a mountain of CVs.

All this time the directors were still insistent that we should tell no one that the Unit existed! Quite how this was to happen I was unsure, especially as by now there was a slow trickle of staff who just happened to pass by our ever expanding offices.

The bubble quickly burst when The Daily Mail ran a front-page headline, "L&G Mis-Selling Scandal!".

I think a couple of directors resigned on the spot, which we were very pleased about as they were really getting in the way! All holidays were automatically cancelled and nobody could have any time off for any reason.

Believe it or not other parts of Kingswood were still making staff redundant. However, L&G in their kindness allowed these poor ex-employees to use a room in the Kingswood offices to send off their CVs and make phone calls etc.

Hearing about this I did a slow walk past their room and then back the other way. There were some excellent people there including a few who had been in my pantos! They all very quickly became part of our growing Empire. Once again see how drama (pantos anyway) and work played an interesting role.

Someone then realised that we hadn't designed and programmed a computer system to deal with the 'mis-selling scandal'. I was given the task to go and find some programmers. I had absolutely no idea what I was doing! Thankfully I found a suitable external company who charged us £1,000 per day per member of their staff. That was a great deal of money in the early 1990s.

I became very experienced in interviewing potential external staff. I have no idea how many interviews I carried out, but it must have easily been over a thousand.

I used the new coffee lounge for interviews as I found that applicants were more at ease and, of course, more liable to say the wrong thing.

Talking about 'wrong things' reminds me of a guy I interviewed and accepted for a particular post. The following day the Employment Agency who had originally sent him rang to say that he had lied throughout his interview, especially about his past, but wanted to see me to apologise.

He came back though and, much against my better judgement, I gave him a second chance. To my knowledge he is still working at L&G. It could have been a disaster though, but I guess it is occasionally worth listening to your gut reaction.

I mentioned we used temporary staff for the more routine tasks. At one stage we used 'hot desking', so if someone went home for the day, a temp immediately sat in their place. We also had the 5–9pm shift. A few 'celebs' turned up as temp staff, including several ex-EastEnders actors.

Were there any interesting or funny moments? The short answer is 'no', as everyone including me was far too stressed and overworked.

However, one of the Management Team was a guy, let's call him John, who really should have been some sort of after dinner speaker; he had a whole host of very funny stories.

One day, when even the most experienced staff were starting to shout at each other, John was introduced. He told story after story and soon had everyone in hysterics.

This soon became a Friday lunchtime 'mic special' which everyone looked forward to, subsequently becoming a weekly event. Some of the directors even put in an appearance.

It broke the tension.

John was actually quite a sad story having had several nervous breakdowns. He never made it through to the finale of this project, being signed off long-term sick. You would never have known as he was brilliant at telling stories and was the life and soul of the party.

Come to think of it, there were several interesting facts. One of the external managers I recruited was a guy called 'Oke'. This was not his real name but he was happy to answer to this nickname. His brother is Andy Peters, so we used to get a few inside TV gossip stories.

I had always suffered from a few headaches over the years, but one day while working away at my desk, I really suddenly had an extreme version. Looking back it was probably my first migraine. So, I just carried on, as you do. I was then aware of a young lady, who I had recruited, coming up to me. Very quietly she explained that she was aware that I had a migraine. She promised not to cause any fuss or embarrassment but within a few minutes it would be gone! Apparently, according to my near colleagues, she put her hands about an inch above my head. I could suddenly feel the pain rushing out of my body. In less than a minute, my migraine had gone and so had she. Clearly she had an extraordinary talent and as I later discovered practiced her art for many years. Sometimes I wish she was around now!

After a whirlwind couple of years, I began to think beyond my current role.

Learning Performance was growing rapidly as we were now into the Tony Blair era of "Education, Education, Education", so for once schools actually had some funds!

I was also taking time off to run Learning Performance school workshops. I used to tell everyone that I was redecorating the house. I was quickly getting to the stage where I couldn't remember which room I had decorated, so there was a distinct possibility that I would be found out very soon.

Finally, I really couldn't think of another job at L&G that would remotely match my current role. It was time to take the plunge and leave for another exciting project. Learning Performance Training!

I remember my final day making an 'impromptu' speech to many of those who I had worked with, including a few directors! I received my retirement clock.

I left with a tear or two, but soon cheered up as I left the L&G car park for the final time.

Learning Performance awaited – but that is another story!

Like most things, time changes rapidly.

The building now lies empty, as L&G moved out a couple of years ago. The residents, fearing that if they weren't careful there would be a huge new housing estate, managed somehow to obtain a preservation order on the building! The fight continues, but the building might just be converted into retirement flats – I may yet return!

My Parents' Love Letters

When Heather and I were clearing out 9 The Close, we discovered a large bundle of letters tied up with red ribbon at the back of one of their bedroom drawers. It is never an easy job to sort and remove clothing, furniture and loads of knick-knacks which once meant so much to my parents.

My Father was, by this time, living with us at Number 4, while my Mother was residing in a nursing home.

To be honest, I don't think we even looked at the letters until some considerable time later.

Although I have always referred to them as my parents' love letters, as it turned out they were, in reality, my Mother's letters to my Father. There was no sign of his replies! However, I think it is reasonably safe to say that as the letters were tied up with ribbon, it is very likely that my Mother kept her own letters.

The 'love' letters were more about life and times in the late 1920s and early '30s, with mentions of West End Shows they saw together which were fun to research on Google.

Well let's start at the very beginning. Auntie Mabel (my Father's sister) somehow arranged for my Father to sit next to my Mother at the Stagers Annual Dinner and Dance held in 1928. Mabel was living in Croydon at the time and was an active member of the Stagers. I vaguely remember visiting their house, with an old-fashioned range in the kitchen, which we sat around to keep warm. However I digress, this devious seating arrangement clearly worked, as they immediately started seeing each other even though my Father lived in Hove! He did though, own a car, which was relatively unusual and a great status symbol. So, he must have cut quite a dash with his stylish clothes and 'with-it' car. My Mother would have been living with her parents in Addiscombe and must have been impressed. Their first few letter exchanges kept mentioning that they must be 'careful'! Apart from the more obvious meaning we finally discovered, several letters later, what they were so worried about; my Father also had another girl in tow, in fact he was currently engaged to her!! The little devil.

So, whether Mabel did not like his fiancée, we can only guess, but I fail to see any other reason for setting up the blind date. Now in those days, a girl could still sue for 'breach of promise', although I am unsure what they would have gained by doing so – financial reward? Anyway, Mabel's husband Don knew someone (I assume a Solicitor), who soon put an end to that idea.

I found it strange that this event was never ever referred to by any Starbucks, least of all by my Mother.

Well, back to how the letters reflected life in the late 1920s.

For example, there are a number of instances where my Mother said she needed to finish a letter to my Father so she could catch the last post, which was apparently 9.30pm from Addiscombe and this was a local post box. I believe it was sometimes possible to send a letter first thing in the morning and receive a reply by 'close-of-play' the same day. What a great postal system we had in those days!

My Mother referred to the musical she was currently involved in at Stagers, with a brief look at how well or badly rehearsals were progressing.

In the 1920s the UK, and I guess London in particular, often suffered from dense fog, known as smog. This was of course caused by pollution. My Mother mentions coming out of the West Croydon rehearsal hall and having to join hands with both friends and strangers in order to find their way to East Croydon station, which was a mile or so away. The phrase, "I can't see my hand in front of my face", was very true of that time.

Talk about young things around town, I have a great picture of my Mother and Father plus a few friends, walking along Brighton seafront looking very debonair in all the latest gear.

As time progressed in their 'courtship', there is a lovely romantic moment described in one of the letters, of the two of them watching the sun come up from their car on Brighton seafront. They then drove back to Croydon (not a quick 45-minute journey in 1930) and my Mother going off to work in London – wow! They were clearly very much in love during their two years together, so they decided to get married. This was a quick romance as engagement sometimes went on for many years in those far off days.

Although my Father's letter to my grandparents has not survived, their reply giving permission for their only daughter to marry is in my possession. This is almost the only letter I have from my grandparents apart from a 'Wee Willie Winkie' postcard!

There are a few 'raunchy' letters, but here is probably not the correct place to reveal everything.

I do have all the letters and a few photos and plan to place them into a book format some day.

A fabulous historical timeline of events and most important their blossoming love for each other.

I feel I now know my parents a little better. After all, not many people get to see their parents love letters!

My Parents

As I recall my childhood memories, I am struck by how many times my Father gets a mention! I really don't mean this unkindly, but my overall impression during my early years was my Mother's undoubted influence.

My Mother features everywhere but I suspect this is difficult to quantify in specific terms.

My Father was always a lady's man, flirting and chatting up the pretty girls everywhere he went.

This made me feel really embarrassed during my teenage years.

I became a very reluctant and poor stage dancer after joining Stagers (more about this later). But I was terrified to touch any of the girl dancers, which is impossible to achieve when rehearsing a musical. Later I got over this problem! Or was it just my growing-up phase?

My Mother constantly criticised my Father during my formative years. Mostly about changing his job. For years he worked for the Danish Bacon Company (DBC) as a sales representative. His basic role was to visit the many food shops in his London territory selling as much produce as possible. The DBC sold a great deal more than just bacon. It was, of course, long before the rise of the supermarket chains. Sometimes this worked in our favour; as for many years he often brought home a large joint of ham, which would last most of the week.

My Mother always wanted him to better himself by moving on to another company in a similar line of business, and I suspect at a higher salary. He was 'bullied' at work by a Mr Sparrow, who I thought must have looked like a bird! Actually, I think Mr Sparrow was my Father's boss and clearly wanted higher productivity and turnover.

I think there were a few 'works' outings to Margate when I was small. The DBC also had a 'Bring your Child to Work Day' long before they became part of the current work ethos. I met Mr Sparrow, who actually didn't look at all like a sparrow; he was smarmy though.

At the time, my Father's area included Soho. He always told my Mother that he had an agreement with the 'girls' not to hassle him; I am not sure she totally believed him! Anyway, during my office visit when we passed through Soho girl after girl shouted out, "Hello Ted". My Father said he didn't know how they had found out his name!

Changing the mood a little, I remember my Mother always coming into my room every night before she went to bed. I guess she must have been praying for me. I used to pretend I was asleep. My Father snored at about 1,000 decibels. So maybe she was just delaying going to bed!

My Mother could sometimes put the 'fear of God' into people, especially those who didn't always agree with her. Vivien, my first wife, was always at a permanent disadvantage, never ever being able to win her around. I don't think they particularly liked each other, so I tended to get the flack.

On the other hand, Mum could be fun and clearly enjoyed the company of her friends. I can remember evenings, usually with Stager friends, which always ended up with a sing-song.

Stagers suddenly found a pianist, who was actually rather good. He could sight read and play anything that was requested. We had some brilliant sing-alongs at our house, as he made my piano sound like a Steinway!

However, someone found out he was a homosexual. The committee met and he was immediately asked to leave the Croydon Stagers. He was also banned from any future sing-alongs. I found this very sad and can remember how upset he was at the time. Guess it was the late 1950s and homosexuality was still illegal. How times have changed.

My Mother was Stagers' secretary since time began, totally dominating all committee meetings, but as she was one of the very few who did any work, she was more than tolerated.

Once my Father retired, he came into his own. He had a number of part-time jobs, which included travelling on trains throughout Europe as a courier (I don't think he necessarily knew where he was, but his personality and gift of the gab got him through). He also ran a small shop for staff within the British Rail Building, which was then situated in CROYDON! Not only selling confectionery, but snacks, teas and coffees etc.

A few years ago, Carrie and I started up a conversation with this random guy on a train destined for Selhurst Park (I wonder where we might have been going?). Anyway, it turned out that he worked for British Rail and remembered both the shop and my Father.

It's a small world.

My Mother also worked in various offices. I vaguely remembered her working for one of the Palace managers in the 1950s – maybe Cyril Spiers?

She also worked for a period of time at the Royal Society for Prevention of Accidents (ROSPA), which used to be located in the old round VW building at Purley Oaks. You may remember the Tufty books.

Later in their retirement, they took themselves off on various holidays abroad, which included long vacations in America and Canada. After one such vacation, my Father came home with a very violent sickness bug and fever and was quickly transferred to the isolation hospital in Waddon. When I visited him there was a notice outside his room which read 'possible typhoid'. Thankfully it wasn't.

Their great, shared passion was Fairfield Halls, an arts and entertainment centre in Croydon. When the Halls first opened a voluntary body of stewards was set up to run the front of house and, when necessary, look after visiting stars. A similar organisation was set up for the lady programme sellers which my Mother joined; I think they got some sort of commission dependent on the number of programmes sold.

The grand opening of Fairfield Halls took place in 1962 and was a glittering occasion. The Queen Mother was in the Royal Box, having officially opened the Halls. There was a classical concert by the London Philharmonic Orchestra, conducted by the world-famous Sir Malcolm Sargent. I remember the actual concert was a bit of a bore, but I went with my '16 going on 17' girl.

Our joy was to watch the Queen Mother giving a coy wave to Sir Malcolm Sargent, who waved back even though he was conducting at the time. Afterwards there was a reception where both my parents were introduced to the Queen Mother. I think we had to wait outside as, after all, we were mere commoners! Some years later, my parents were invited to the Queen's Garden Party in recognition of my Mother's services to amateur theatre. Although they loved the experience, they came away starving, each having received just one quarter of a cucumber sandwich.

Sadly, in later life, my Mother lost her battle with Alzheimer's disease.

It was sad to watch my intelligent Mother slowly degenerate until she was unable to remember her husband. My Father never quite understood how this could happen and was visibly upset, particularly as she appeared still to remember me! She spent around nine years in various nursing homes. However, more about my Mother's final years later.

My Father remained active even though he had suffered a heart attack. He had come across to us and Heather sat him in a chair and immediately called the GP and also called me to come home from work at Kingswood. When I got home Dad was saying he wasn't feeling that well and his lips were blue. The GP had already arrived and called an ambulance, so I went with my Father to the hospital. After several hours in A&E he was transferred to a ward. However, the following morning after his heart attack I found him not comatose in bed, but walking around the hospital ward chatting to everyone.

Typical of my Father.

The doctor in charge told me that he was easily the oldest in the ward, but clearly the brightest and most alert. He was, by then, in his mid-70s. More concerning was that the doctors were convinced that he had already suffered previous heart attacks – what! However, he made an excellent recovery and went back to stewarding and having an active life.

Sadly, one weekend while he was visiting his sister Mabel in Hove, he never made it to her Hove Nursing Home. The home rang to say my Father hadn't arrived which was a worry, as he was always on time. Ringing the hotel where he had stayed the previous night, I almost knew that he had died.

The lady receptionist answered and immediately said she would go to his room. However, I insisted that it should only be the Hotel Manager. A few minutes later, I took the dreaded call from the Hotel Manager. My 'daddy' had died peacefully sitting in an armchair with the TV on. Not a bad way to go I suppose.

Sometimes at a funeral you gain a vivid but fleeting image which remains with you for many years. From inside the funeral car as we were slowly driven up to the Crematorium, all I could see was a long line of men with their hands clasped in front of them. I immediately became aware that these were my Father's fellow stewards who had all come to pay their respects; it was clear they had been very fond of him. There is something about men, probably all in their 70s, immaculately turned out in dark overcoats, white shirts and black ties. Mind you, they told me some amazing stories after the funeral!

My Parents had a good life together although, like most marriages, there were hiccups along the way.

My parents told me that they went up to London on VE Day and did the 'Lindy Hop' around Trafalgar Square, along with thousands of others; and they waved at the Queen!

To me, they were great parents who were, I like to think, very proud of their son.

My Life as a Fairfield Halls Steward

I joined the voluntary band of stewards in 1962, probably for three reasons. I suspect because both my parents were involved and, more importantly, I could get a lift back home each night. But most of all, I could see all the plays, musicals and visiting stars for free; I couldn't wait.

The stars of that era included Matt Monro, Morecambe and Wise, The Rolling Stones, Gerry and the Pacemakers, Dusty Springfield and The Beatles.

I will always remember The Beatles' visit. It was immediately after their first hit 'Please Please Me' had leapt up the charts; so they were still relatively unknown. There was absolutely no security, as no one guessed what was to come over the coming weeks, months and years.

Here were four Liverpool lads attempting to play their music to a full house of screaming girls. Their screaming was so loud that I don't think I regained my hearing until two days later. The Beatles couldn't hear themselves play, as these were the days before earpieces. They had to stop in the middle of several songs, as they just couldn't hear the rest of the group.

Girls were constantly fainting, being carried out by the St John Ambulance staff, coming round, rushing back to their seats, only to faint again! Ringo bizarrely had part of the audience sitting behind him in what was normally the choir stalls. The girls were rushing down stealing his drumsticks until he had none at all! I remember him rushing into the audience to retrieve them so that he could carry on playing. He was strangely using The Dakotas' drum kit; they were meant to be the support group but failed to turn up. Jelly Babies were being thrown as Paul had earlier made the unfortunate mistake of saying he liked them. These were followed by panties and bras.

Then most of the audience were up and as one charged the stage! The look of absolute fear on The Beatles' faces still haunts me – well occasionally anyway. I became involved with other stewards to form a line in front of the stage to repel those who were intent on storming the stage.

After the show we all retired to the Artists' Bar at the rear of the Halls each with our own story to tell. Suddenly there was a frantic call from the backstage doorman saying that hundreds of girls had not only taken down the iron gates in the artists' car park but were now storming the back doors of the concert hall. We all rushed down to hold the barricades (the back doors). There must have been around 400 girls going absolutely crazy.

We then noticed the four Beatles standing quietly to one side looking scared witless. Somehow, we managed to get them to their car. However, their car was then rocked back and forth by the crowd. The police finally arrived but refused to get out of their car! Finally, the Beatles' car managed to get away running over a couple of stewards on the way; luckily no one was seriously hurt. For all future 'pop' concerts, there was a deep pit in front of the stage plus an army of 'bouncers' who normally worked at the various CROYDON bars.

In complete contrast was Dusty Springfield, singing her heart out during a matinée performance in the Concert Hall. She would then go on to perform at her evening concert some two hours later. Strangely we found her sitting in the foyer rather than her dressing room between performances; she was happy to chat to anyone and everyone, including me. I thought then that despite her fame, she was in fact very lonely.

Matt Monro was also a visitor during 1963, playing in front of two sell-out performances. He was known as 'The Man with the Golden Voice'. Sadly, a few years later he became an alcoholic, although this was already apparent during his visit. Once again, I was in the Artists' Bar having a cup of tea(!) whilst he sank pint after pint, between shows. You would never have known, as his performance and vocals were both superb. He recorded the theme song 'From Russia with Love' for the James Bond film of the same name.

Acker Bilk and his Paramount Jazz Band were another group to visit. I was horrified to hear wrong note after wrong note at the start of their show. However, one by one they wandered off stage to return with a pint of beer. This was topped up by various audience members. The result was a fabulous second half with not a wrong note played or heard.

I also watched Morecambe and Wise perform their show which, in my eyes, was a little disappointing. This turned out to be their only show filmed live in front of the cameras. Whether it was the TV lights or cameras and trailing cables that didn't help the atmosphere, they seemed strangely subdued. They had a great opening though, coming out from one side of the Concert Hall Stage to a standing ovation, bowing in the middle and then walking straight off the other side!

One evening, Sir Winston Churchill visited the Ashcroft Theatre to see his daughter Sarah perform in a play. By this time, he was old and very infirm, so he sat in the front row of the stalls. At the end he was raised up by lift to stage level. Sarah wept in his arms, as they had not spoken for a number of years, then he was gone, giving his famous 'V for victory' salute. He died about six months later. You could say that I had met Sir Winston Churchill!

Occasionally I was asked if I would like to earn a few pounds as a Followspot Operator, usually in the Concert Hall. It's very hot work as the back heat from the powerful beam is directly aimed at your chest. You also have to concentrate the entire time so as not to miss your cues, not to mention wear gloves as the metal surround gets very hot. Things have, of course, changed for the better these days.

On one such occasion I was a Followspot Operator for Shirley Bassey! There was lighting and sound rehearsal in the morning, followed by two sell-out shows. As she paced out her moves around the stage, I was being yelled at through my headphones about my various cues for her concert. Suddenly Shirley Bassey was also literally screaming at me, calling me every swear word under the sun, including a few I had never previously heard before or since. I had lost concentration, resulting in her being plunged into darkness. Hence her rant. She must have stood ranting at me for what seemed like five long minutes. Then there was deafening silence. Needless to say, I followed her every move throughout both shows almost shaking with fear.

There is however a happy ending to my story. She left a red rose for me at the end of her final show with a note saying, "to the best Followspot Operator in town!". I went home a very happy boy. I pressed the rose and kept it for many years, fool that I am.

The most exciting concert was, believe it or not, the regular Children's Concert which was held most Saturday mornings. Leonard Bernstein (of West Side Story fame) was due to perform a classical concert at the Halls the same evening. Normally the children's concerts were extremely boring and likely to put them off classical music for life. However, someone had the bright idea of inviting Bernstein and his 120-piece (I counted) New York Philharmonic Orchestra to play for the children's morning concert.

West Side Story first appeared in the later 1950s, so I suspect everyone in that audience knew every song. Bernstein started with 'Peter and Wolf' ... or tried to start. All 1,500 kids started chanting, "We want West Side Story". Eventually he stopped trying to play and turned to his audience and again asked them what they wanted him to play. I guess he sort of knew what was going to happen as by chance each musician already had a copy of the overture on their music stands!

To hear a 120-piece orchestra play West Side Story was something to behold. His audience just swayed and sang every song. For what was meant to be an encore he chose the one number Bernstein knew they all wanted to hear 'America!'. To hear 'America' played by such a large orchestra, which included around eight drums and percussion players, still makes the hairs on my arm stand up and gives me goose bumps all over.

The kids were out of the seats singing and dancing around the stage. Bernstein then asked if those in the balcony would like to come down and join in. So, we had 1,500 kids singing and dancing along with us stewards, the parents who had come to collect their children and anyone else that wanted to join in. I'm not sure how many times he played 'America', but it must have been six at the very least.

What was meant to be the usual one hour children's morning concert lasted over two hours and nobody cared or wanted to go home? What an atmosphere!

I was also on duty for the classical Bernstein concert held that same evening. Bernstein informed the audience that his morning concert was one of the most memorable and exciting he and his orchestra had ever played. He would never forget that morning. I certainly haven't!

I enjoyed my few short years as a steward, meeting a great many stars of the 1960s.

Oh, and I showed people to their seats as well.

Vivien

This is a difficult chapter to write and I thought long and hard as to whether I should even include a few words on the subject of my first wife, as this still brings back painful memories which I had long since thought I had successfully suppressed.

However, on reflection this does form part of my life so I finally decided to write down a few salient points relating to these difficult years. Nick, I am sorry if you are upset by any of the following but please remember this is entirely from my perspective.

I first met Vivien at Legal and General, where she worked only a few yards down the corridor from me. Our first date was at the old Astoria Cinema in Purley, now long-since demolished.

After a few months she left L&G and trained to become a Primary School Teacher at the Training College near Bromley in Kent. After the first year of training Vivien shared a house with two other girls and their boyfriends. I still exchange Christmas cards with them.

After Vivien qualified, she taught at Hayes Lane Primary School in Kenley. One morning a couple of years later Vivien woke up one morning at my parents' house unable to put her feet on the ground.

This was diagnosed as rheumatoid arthritis, which slowly spread to the rest of her body ending up in her fingers. For some years she went to a specialist at Guy's Hospital in London.

Vivien was given a huge variety of drugs, only some of which were helpful. Her fingers, although still usable, became very distorted.

Taking a step or two back, Vivien's parents divorced when she was in her teens. I don't think I ever quite understood her various relatives, although I can now use the excuse that this was over 50 years ago. Unfortunately she became, over the following years, increasingly obsessed with her half-sister, who had sadly died when only 40 years of age. She was certain that would happen to her at the same age.

Our wedding took place in April 1968 at Christchurch, Purley. We were married by the Bishop of Ascot. He was one of Vivien's half relatives, the Grange–Bennetts. After the reception at a pub in South Croydon, my best man (another guy from the Stagers with two left feet) drove us to London where we caught the overnight train to Bude in Cornwall. A sleeper was out of the question financially, so we sat up all night. This would have been OK, except there were two nuns sat opposite who stared at us for most of the journey!

I am sure there were good times during our marriage, but sadly I don't remember them.

As Vivien became more difficult to handle, I had absolutely no idea how to understand or how to respond.

Then along came the only good thing. Our son, Nick, was born at Purley Hospital on April 4th 1971. He was a relatively small baby weight-wise, so was immediately transferred to Mayday Hospital in Croydon. Vivien followed on a week later. Things did not improve that much after we left hospital and I spent many hours feeding and looking after baby Nick during the following months, as Vivien was very depressed.

When we were first married, we moved to Oaks Road, Kenley where the terraced house cost the grand total of £4,000! Later we moved to Brancaster Lane. I remember it poured with rain on the day of the move. By this time, I was on a very heavy dosage of sleeping pills, but was still getting up to Nick during the night. Things seemed to go from bad to worse.

I became suspicious she was seeing someone else.

One Christmas my parents came around on Boxing Day for a meal, only to be served a salad with Vivien saying she needed some air. She did not return for several hours.

A few weeks later, Vivien was playing principal boy in the local Sanderstead panto. I went to a matinée performance with Nick, only to find that she was the worse for drink on stage and her dressing room was filled with flowers, not sent from me!

A couple of weeks later I came back from work to find an empty house. She had left with Nick and gone to live with a man called Derek Dixon, taking all the furniture and Nick's things with her. Even worse she had not said where she was going and she had my son. I did not know where they were for another week and, in despair, sat in the lounge by the phone all day and night.

The strange thing was I kind of knew him, having watched his musical performances as a small boy with the Stagers. I had also seen him when taking Taffy for a walk as a teenager, as he was going out with a girl who lived around the corner from The Close.

He was married at the time.

The Aftermath

Vivien leaving hit me harder than I would have imagined. I took myself off to Samaritans, where I met a lovely old lady who was extremely deaf! So not the best possible starts. Later I learnt that two Stager girls who were trained Samaritans had seen me coming up the path and sent the deaf lady to chat to me. Apparently, you cannot offer advice to someone you know.

I also tried a marriage guidance counsellor who worked from a large house in Coulsdon. The counsellor was excellent and later suggested that Vivien should also attend. Apparently it did not go well according to the counsellor, who told me that I was much better off without her! Not a very professional approach but probably a true reflection.

Over the following months, Vivien informed me that she had made a terrible mistake and wanted to come back to me. Like a fool, I agreed. Almost immediately, she fell sick and I had to call the doctor.

Four days later I again came back to an empty house.

I subsequently learnt that the doctor had asked her what the hell she was doing back at Brancaster Lane. Hardly very professional to say the least. He was a young, very stylish doctor who drove around in a sports car usually with a pretty girl in a headscarf next to him. He was the junior partner to the doctor I normally saw.

I immediately visited my doctor and after I had told him what his junior partner had said he burst into his colleagues consulting room. All I could hear was a shouting match, things being thrown and what sounded like a fight.

I left.

Later I learnt that my doctor had immediately terminated the partnership and actually thrown the guy out of the building. Some months later, the local paper reported that the young doctor had been struck off for this and other similar complaints.

Vivien became more and more dependent on drink so I shielded Nick as best I could; this was difficult as he lived mainly with her and only came to live with me whenever she was ill. Many years later, when Nick was a young adult, he came to live with my parents to get away from his Mother's drinking.

Eventually I realised that the marriage breakdown was not all my fault and I started to rebuild my life. Some years later Vivien sadly died from drink-related problems.

I really don't want to talk about this anymore – sorry Nick.

Then along came Heather …

Heather

Heather and I first met in 1975, in the auditorium of the Ashcroft Theatre at Fairfield Halls, during a live performance of a rock opera. I was performing in the rock musical 'Two Gentlemen of Verona' as a knight in full armour.

The production involved the cast coming into the audience selecting, or at the very least encouraging, someone to dance with us. This could sometimes prove difficult, so we usually pulled out friends of ours or someone else in the cast mentioned a friend of theirs in a certain row.

So this is how I met Heather, seated in row AA20 on the Friday night of 'Two Gents'.

I liked what I saw, so between the Saturday matinée and the evening performance, I plucked up the courage to ring and ask her out.

We met the following week for a Chinese and kissed for the first of many, many times on the rooftop car park of the VW building in Purley Oaks. Very romantic.

Heather had an MG sports car which was very trendy but tended to break down, a lot, let in the rain and was very drafty.

Heather spent a great deal of time at Brancaster Lane. She was then living with three other girls in a rented house in Whyteleafe. I picked up the local director of a Stagers play one night and drove past Heather on her way up Whyteleafe Hill. I think even then I had the feeling that we would get married. Mind you it nearly didn't happen! Heather had Suki, a big persian cat who backed me into the corner of her bedroom snarling with her claws at the ready the first time we met.

Heather took me to meet her parents who lived at the time in Chandlers Ford. Her Mum (Jean) welcomed me with open arms, and her Dad (David) was easy to talk to. However Graeme, Heather's younger brother, was far more suspicious and no wonder after Heather's disastrous first marriage. In fact, we both had disastrous first marriages for very different reasons.

At that time, Nick used to come and see us on alternate weekends, so it was natural to take him on a holiday to Butlin's Bognor Regis with Heather, my parents, not to mention myself. This was before we married, so Heather and I had separate bedroom chalets with Nick sharing with me. After lights out at night I crept along to Heather's bedroom. Later I would creep back past my parents' chalet to where Nick and I were sleeping. My Father said that my Mother used to count the minutes I was with Heather!

About six months after we met, in the March 1975, we moved in together. It was decided that Heather should sell her beloved MG Sports car and just rely on my Morris Minor, so I knew she was seriously in love with me!

My Mother used to come round to the house just to make sure we were OK!

Once she arrived with my Father on a Sunday afternoon. We were upstairs at the time with a few of Heather's clothes scattered up the stairs. My Mother was shocked as I think she thought I would go blind, while my Father did all he could not to laugh.

Before I met Heather my Mother often used to leave a dinner for me on the front doorstep; it took her a few months to realise that this service was no longer needed.

Or am I being too nice?

In January of 1976 we decided that we would like to get married. No need to wait so we booked the Croydon Registry Office for 20th March. For us this was the natural progression, although probably we decided sooner rather than later was the best way forward as we were madly in love!

Heather is the best thing that has ever happened to me. Kind, considerate, calm and loving. A great sense of humour and a joy to be with. The only negative I can think of is that Heather doesn't like football!

Even some 40 plus years later her voice over the phone still makes me 'tingle' with pleasure. Never could anyone be as lucky as me to have such a wonderful wife. Maybe we appreciated each other more after both coming out of disastrous previous relationships. It is not really worth thinking about other possible reasons, as we were both clearly made for each other. I love you Heather and I always will.

Heather and I were both rather poor financially as a result of our recent divorces. We married at Croydon Registry Office. It was a small intimate affair with both our parents plus Heather's grandmother, her sister Carol and her husband John and their three boys, Uncle Bertie and Vye, Graeme and his then girlfriend, and ourselves! Oh yes, and Pat and Alan Yardley turned up to wish us well.

Our wedding photos were taken in the Town Hall gardens and then we went on for lunch at the then local Harvester in Coulsdon. Our Honeymoon was spent in Bournemouth at the Legal & General flats which they let out to staff. They were reasonably OK, a little shabby with old furniture but we really didn't care that much as we were very much in love and it was very cheap! However we had just about enough money to treat ourselves to a posh hotel for the first night!

Strangely while on Honeymoon, Heather saw her ex-husband drive past. Despite living on a shoestring we decided to become pregnant as soon as we could; Heather fell pregnant by Christmas.

To earn extra money over the coming years, we had a succession of part time jobs.

I was a Littlewoods Pools Collector, which involved going around your 'region' of houses collecting both money and coupons. It seemed to be both cold and pouring with rain on most collection nights. Heather became a 'Dapergem' Jewellery party plan girl, holding or going to various houses to show off their priceless stock. It was similar to Tupperware parties which, come to think of it, Heather was also an agent for.

However, perhaps she was best known as the Avon lady. I was known as the 'bearded Avon lady', as I sold plenty of stock visiting the various typing pools at L&G.

We were also involved in shows together at both the Ashcroft and the Miller Centre, plus Sanderstead Pantos. We became members of the Times Theatre Club, which meant we were able to see mostly musicals at cheaper prices.

On one occasion, we went on to a Night Club, where we saws several of the principals from the show we had just seen. No idea how we got home?

During all this, and despite being a new mother herself, one of the really difficult things that Heather had to deal with was my ex-wife, Vivien, who remarried at a similar time to us. On occasions Vivien was not a happy person, having (I think) thought the grass would be greener in her new life.

Heather dealt with her brilliantly, being both patient and understanding. My ex-wife mostly rang to complain about her new husband. Thank you once again for your patience Heather.

Occasionally I had Vivien's husband Derek on the phone, sometimes in tears, about what she had said to him. In the cold light of day, it was as though Vivien was reading from a script, as many of her words were almost identical to what she had said to me. All very strange.

As time progressed Nick used to turn up in old 'hand-me-down' clothes, I assume from the very worst of charity shops. The very annoying thing was that I paid child maintenance on a regular monthly basis to my ex-wife. Clearly it was not always being used on Nick. So, we often had to spend money on some decent clothes for him. We didn't necessarily resent this, but there wasn't the spare cash around our end either.

Not only did Nick visit at weekends but throughout his formative years he sometimes lived with us for a length of time when things became difficult for Vivien.

I think the first time this happened was towards the end of being pregnant with David, Heather gave up the baby's planned nursery so that Nick could stay. I took leave from work to look after Nick for the fortnight Heather was in hospital to have David by C-section. When Heather was back home she coped with a newborn and Nick for the next three weeks, before

Vivien felt well enough for him to return to her. No wonder I have undying admiration for Heather.

As most will be aware David, Jamie and Richie came along in relatively quick succession, with two years between each wonderful son.

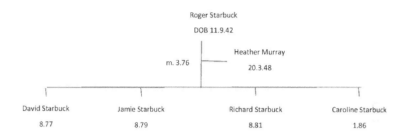

Roger Starbuck
DOB 11.9.42

Heather Murray

m. 3.76

20.3.48

David Starbuck   Jamie Starbuck   Richard Starbuck   Caroline Starbuck

8.77   8.79   8.81   1.86

So, the night feeds started along with a seemingly inability of all our children to go to sleep before the 11pm mark. In those days there were no commercial stations, no Netflix or Amazon, just the good old BBC which closed down every night at 11pm with the National Anthem and a formal, "goodnight, sleep well!". In fact, a full daytime schedule didn't happen until 1980!

Except we usually didn't sleep! As Heather was breastfeeding and 'on duty' for the night-time feeds, I was assigned the late evening shift. Usually walking up and down the dining room with a baby, looking out of the window of Brancaster Lane to see if there was a light on in any other window. Or was I the only one up in the entire world! Sometimes it could feel like that.

Fortunately for us, we were friendly with a young couple who also had a new baby. Now their baby would not sleep unless being driven around Purley, waking up as soon as the engine stopped! So they used to turn up regularly, leave the engine running while nipping in for a quick chat. It was so great to see that there were actually other people awake at midnight and into the small hours of the following morning! Looking back, we both loved the baby and early years bit – really, we did.

In all Heather had four caesareans, which in those days meant Heather had to stay in hospital for around 10 days after each birth, the positive being that she could use this time to rest, recover and bond with each baby.

Times changed rapidly as far as I was concerned. For David's birth, you still had to pace up and down in the 'Father's room', except I didn't. A very nice orderly asked if I would like to stand at the back of the operating room as long as I made absolutely no noise and did not faint! However, the 'matron' noticed as we came out of the Operating Room with cries of, "who let him in?". Everyone, including me, kept very quiet.

For Jamie's birth, we had pre booked the C-section for 2nd August and Heather had gone into Mayday the afternoon before to be ready for the operation. She was given her last meal at 5pm and promptly went into labour about 6pm; panic stations as no theatre free! Heather kept asking for them to phone to tell me, but they never did. So I came along with flowers etc. just in time to see her being wheeled away to theatre, as they had cancelled another op to make way for her. I had to dump the flowers and race after her.

The downside for Heather was that she never saw each baby until, sometimes, a few hours later as she was of course under anaesthetic. So, for Richard's birth, Heather was brave enough to stay awake using the new epidural injected into the spine. Finally getting to cuddle a newborn, but he had breathing difficulties because he was four weeks early and went off to spend his first 24 hours in intensive care!!

Strangely after one birth I was taken by a nurse and shown the 'afterbirth'; which as I tried not to faint was apparently very healthy.

Our last baby was Carrie, born four years after Richie. She should have been born on 29th December, but Heather developed a cold over Christmas and the doctors thought it best to wait until the cold had cleared up before putting Heather under anaesthetic. She showed no sign of wanting to come out, so they booked a planned C-section for 9.30am on 14th January 1986. I had to get the boys off to school so I was running a bit late getting there. Cries of, "hurry up" came from the hospital team, before I was quickly gowned up and there I was in the Operating Theatre again. All I could hear was the team giving the anaesthetist their lunch orders while they operated. I wanted to yell, 'that's my wife you have there' but decided to keep quiet, fearing that they might get the lunch order wrong (it's a joke Heather).

However, there were a few things not to like during this time such as nappy buckets, nappies to clean etc; there were no such things as disposables.

So, what else happened while we lived at Brancaster Lane.

Well there was the girl up the road who suddenly discovered her 'husband' was a bigamist. So she wasn't married to him at all. He somehow kept two families running at the same time.

Then there was Peter and Pam next door. He really was a strange guy who somehow married a lovely wife.

A particular mention to a very young Jamie, who 'accidentally' sprayed Peter in the garden with our hose. Peter came straight round to sort him out. Peter didn't seem to realise that he had to get past me first so never made it anywhere near Jamie.

No sense of humour whatsoever.

After we left to live at 4 The Close, Peter had a legal dispute with the new owners of our old house. I was called as a reluctant witness, even though it really was only about a foot of land. Ridiculous!

Years later Heather saw Pam working in the local library and, what a surprise, they were no longer together. Then, of course, there was Harry and Ella who lived on the other side of us. They were the really nice neighbours.

Harry was an ex-RAF Officer having served mostly abroad. They often had their meals outside even when it was really cold. Ella was secretary to Lady Astor, while Harry had turned his attention to writing children's books. The really great positive was Harry's prize vegetable patch. This was situated at the far end of our garden. Apparently, Harry had negotiated a deal with the previous owners. So, we were more than happy for him to continue as Harry provided us with vegetables and fruit galore.

Oh and David at six weeks old developed projectile vomiting, which was quickly solved once diagnosed, with a small operation for pyloric stenosis. Frightening at the time though, especially as poor David managed to project at an ever-increasing distance. When we finally arrived at the Children's Hospital in Carshalton, the doctor was insistent that a nurse should feed David to make sure the diagnosis from the GP was correct. When David threw up, the nurse nearly dropped him!

While on the subject, David was sadly bitten just above his eye. This was Sacha, Vivien and Nick's dog, which she had somehow managed to persuade us to take on.

Another rush to Carshalton Children's Hospital. After checking that his eyeball was thankfully not damaged, stitches were required. However, the surgeon was not on site and had to come by pedal bike! So, there was an obvious delay. The surgeon, on his arrival, decided that he could not anesthetise David due to his then heart murmur. So a nurse plus me had to hold David down while the surgeon stitched him up. That was bad enough but there was a problem, Heather fainted! So, I was stretched over David to make certain he didn't move. Strangely I was ice cool, although normally quite squeamish at all hospital-related things. I remember shaking when it was all over, along with Heather, who just couldn't watch.

Happy days!

Another thing, the house in Brancaster Lane was definitely haunted. I always thought there was something or someone behind me on the staircase. I don't think it was a particularly nasty ghost though.

I have previously alluded to the problems we had with my ex-wife and her husband, Derek. Or rather the problems Heather in particular had, mainly with Vivien during the day when I was at work. However, on one memorable occasion we took a phone call from both of them absolutely desperate for financial help. Derek had been fired from yet another job selling kitchen equipment. He had sold the demonstration model!

Idiots that we probably were, we went round to see both of them the following day. But somehow or other their blind panic had overnight turned into a non-problem.

I remember thinking that was the last time I would allow my poor, lovely wife to become involved in a face-to-face meeting with them.

Well back to Brancaster Lane. My Mother was becoming increasingly difficult for my Father to handle as we found that she had become doubly incontinent ...

4 The Close

In 1988 we decided to move to The Close to be near both of my parents. Luckily for us, 4 The Close was up for sale. So, for roughly the following two years, Heather looked, and cleared up, after my Mother. My Father didn't quite understand why his wife was functioning so poorly.

I suspect some of my readers (maybe my only readers?) will remember the Sunday afternoon teas, including trifle and cakes not to mention bread and butter. Where they had previously been happy events, now Heather and I had to watch that no one was going to suffer afterwards from food poisoning. Often the trifle had gone off because it had been made many days prior to our Sunday 'high tea' gathering. Very sad and quite stressful trying to ensure none of our lovely children became ill.

We also had the wonderful Ida who lived next door at 5 The Close. She had been notoriously difficult for many years although my Father and I could, on occasions, 'butter her up'. She loved walking arm in arm with my Father parading around The Close. Ida was someone else for Heather to deal with, although she 'once again' took this in her stride.

For years we always seemed to have difficult neighbours although Terry and Wendy, on the other side of us, were a delight with their dogs and birds. We still receive Christmas cards from them, Terry and Wendy that is!

Soon after we moved in, there was yet another period of wind and rain. We watched the tiles blowing off my parents' roof, with my Father looking out the back door oblivious to the fact that one could land on his head. Most houses (except ours) had some damage. By chance I spotted a roofer working on a property in Pampisford Road and directed him towards The Close. He must have made a fortune over the next couple of days.

My memory of Number 4 was that it was three storeys high with attic bedrooms. A great big lounge with fake beams, which I loved. A separate dining room plus a fair-sized kitchen. The garden, although sloping upwards, was to die for; planted mostly to grass with masses of rose bushes. Difficult to maintain though as the grass and boundary hedging often needed to be cut and the rose beds weeded. There was also a vine in the front garden.

Jamie had always been scared of dogs, having witnessed David being bitten by a dog back at Brancaster Lane. I recall Jamie screaming in the kitchen one day as there was a stray dog loose in our garden. For some reason, soon after this, his previous fear left him and from then on everyone enjoyed having dogs around (I am, however, getting ahead of myself as we didn't have a dog until later).

The downstairs lounge was large enough to have principal cast rehearsals, which included West Side Story. I think Carrie was enthralled on the odd occasion when she was allowed to stay up and watch.

The year after we moved to The Close, my ex-wife Vivien died. Going to her funeral to support Nick was a very strange experience as everyone present I had last seen at our wedding. It is strange how people react. There were a few of her family members who came up to me to say that they had never liked her anyway. A strange thing in my view to say at anyone's funeral. While the couple who had lived on the same road as us just didn't want to talk to me. Divorces and funerals sometimes bring out strange reactions, often from people and friends you least expect.

The next summer my Father had a heart attack, which I have already written about in another chapter. Once released from hospital, he came to live with us camping in the dining room which, to say the least, was hardly ideal. Once again Heather took on yet another member of the Starbuck family, this time my Father.

My parent's house was sold so that the money could be set aside for my Mother's nursing home fees. She had moved out to be cared for in an excellent nursing home some two years before. Within a fortnight she could not remember ever living in The Close. As for my Father, well she really didn't want to know him.

Early in 1992 Heather made contact with John Dibley, the owner of Learning Performance Australia. We had an interview with him and his wife and we were offered the chance to help him develop a UK branch of Learning Performance. He then came to stay, resulting in us purchasing Learning Performance Seminars for the princely sum of just £1. Mind you we paid plenty of royalties to him as the years rolled by as Learning Performance became more and more successful. We did our training with him that summer, and set up admin on a makeshift desk in our bedroom. Some years later, John came across a picture taken in our garden taken at the time of his stay, which I still have.

So, we simply had to move to a bigger house with Heather again being the 'architect', although this was really a very lucky break. By this time, Heather was working part-time at Thomas More School, helping with dyslexic students. She had studied at the Hornsby Centre in 1989 and qualified as a dyslexia therapist. So she could not only help Richie with his dyslexic problems, but teach other children as well.

By chance Heather heard one of the teachers at the photocopier telling a colleague that he really had to urgently move to a smaller property due to financial problems. Heather very quickly suggested that he should look at our house the same evening, while we rushed over to see theirs.

This was at a time of severe recession and no one was buying or selling houses – you guessed it, this amazing coincidence led us to move to 11 Bradmore Way just three weeks later. The quickest and the most stress-free move I have ever experienced!

Both parties couldn't use the same solicitors but found another whose offices were just across the road in Croydon.

Both insurance companies and solicitors all latched onto the urgency of the move, which just shows what can happen compared with the usual three to six months debacle.

Unfortunately, Heather went down with the flu just before the move, so on the actual day of the move things were slightly stressful but only in the short term.

We spent the next 18 years at Bradmore Way; 18 very happy years.

11 Bradmore Way

Things tend to merge into a wild flurry of activities, so here are my memories of our time spent at 11 Bradmore Way, not necessarily in the correct order!

Redecorating and updating the house, which was not in a great state of repair, but had excellent potential.

My Father living in our lounge as a bed-sitting room and his Lada car in our garage.

Saturday mornings spent ferrying all our children around to ballet, piano and swimming lessons; including Jamie walking down the steps at Alan's pool until the water was over his head (sorry Jamie, but the image is still with us).

David walking off up the hill to Coulsdon Sixth Form College. Jamie taking himself off to school on the bus each morning, never being late or missing it. Richie's growing school phobia and finally being 'educated at home'. Carrie growing up from a sweet six-year-old to a lovely young woman. So proud of them all.

Our lovely intelligent dog, Bella, who hated water and would go yards around a puddle rather than get her feet wet. She always seemed to understand everything we said to her. Always positioning her body so you had to step over her to leave the room. Turning her back on us when we left to go on holiday. Bella became seriously ill far too early in her life. She loved going in the car with me; she would sit on the front seat. Sadly, I recall my last car journey with her when she was very ill with her head on my lap. She knew and it still brings a tear to my eye as I write these words.

Heather's Mum coming to live with us after her husband's fatal heart attack in 1999. We had the side glass conservatory and garage converted into a self-contained flat for her.

Cutting the extensive grass. We bought an automatic robot grass cutter, but it kept falling into the holes created by football practice!

All Jamie's friends coming to play football until the grass was just a mud bath. Computer games played for hours by various lads in our dining room, but at least we knew where they were!

The building of the Learning Performance 'office shed' and having our staff use the kitchen and bathroom.

Coming down the outside garden steps and watching the planes fly into the twin towers with Richie. It happened on my birthday, which made celebrating my birthday on that day and for years afterwards almost impossible.

The new pond and waterfall.

Carrie being bullied at several schools. Packing her bags to leave home when she was around 14 years of age with her brothers finding her on the platform at Coulsdon Station and bringing her back.

Susie and Smokie our cats both died, from old age, which made us all very sad.

The arrival of our new next-door neighbours, the Dingles; this really is out of order, as they moved in shortly after us. Miles coming around with his empty plate every time we had a BBQ.

Our neighbour working for Learning Performance both as a presenter and in our office.

My son Nick joining the Learning Performance team working from the 'shed'.

The arrival of Bonnie and Leo, border collie puppies, who promptly started to eat the plaster off our walls and cause general havoc. They grew up into lovely dogs and spent hours on the Downs without ever becoming tired. The collie 'stare' was in evidence as they often spent what seemed like hours playing a game of hide and seek around the car. Sometimes I just walked onto the Downs and they joined me later once one of them had given in. Although they had great temperaments with us, they were not so keen on other dogs; Leo in particular, though he was docile 99% of the time. People that moved were also a potential problem as, being collies, they wanted to nip their ankles to bring them into line! Bonnie given the chance would chase cars. They both came with us when we left Bradmore Way in 2009 but sadly died of old age within a few months of each other in 2019 shortly before we left West Way and moved to Fairfields. They were both 16 years old and I miss them dreadfully.

David at Coulsdon College and then off to university, which turned out to be Aberdeen. Our visits up to Aberdeen by EasyJet at £11.50 return! Before uni David took a gap year travelling to Tanzania, helping to teach at a local school. When he came back I almost missed him at Heathrow as he was so thin and had grown a large bushy beard. David stayed up in Aberdeen after he graduated, buying a house with his then girlfriend. He rang me on his first Christmas Day away from us, from his house, and told us he was very unhappy, having had a row with Catherine.

Nick getting married from our house and travelling to the church in a stretch limo. The only problem being the usual route was blocked by an accident, but we got there with time to spare.

My Father's final heart attack while visiting his sister Mabel in Hove. I remember hearing the news while I was hoovering Jamie's room. Heather and I raced down to the hotel where he had died and collected his car, which we found in a nearby road. We sorted out the undertakers and then I drove back in his car while Heather drove ours. It was raining stair-rods all the way home.

His funeral and then afterwards the 'wake' being held at our house.

Mum-in-Law Jean becoming increasingly frail in both body and mind.

Peter turning up sporadically with various huge lorries. At least he found it easier to park at Bradmore compared to The Close.

Ann coming to our house to massage my back, which I had hurt mowing the lawn. We became firm friends and still meet up, most recently in Portugal. Come to think of it she massaged most of us over many years. I had thought we were a reasonably fit family!?

Buying a fractional share at Quinta da Encosta Velha villa 139 in Portugal. Going to the Euros 2004 to see the England matches played in Lisbon. The journey and food on the coach to and from the matches were just out of this world.

Swimming in our own pool, thinking I never in my wildest dreams thought we would part own such a wonderful villa. Being Chairman of the Fractional Committee at the Resort.

Jamie's having an interview at Watford College for a postgraduate copywriting course, the only trouble being he was abroad on holiday, so he had to fly back via Manchester and then get down to Coulsdon on the overnight coach. Dedication but it worked, Jamie got the place, which started his journey to great things in advertising.

David meeting Dawn when they were both working near us and their fabulous wedding where we all wore kilts; well us men folk did! A great reception; I remember all the dancing. His rapid rise through the teaching ranks, gaining a brilliant job as Deputy Head in Aberdeen.

Heather's two operations for hip replacements, oh and talking of Heather ...

Pheochromocytoma – November 2005

Heather had known for some time that things were not quite right as far as her health and general wellbeing were concerned. She had been diagnosed with type 2 diabetes in 2000.

She had been suffering from high blood pressure and extreme fainting episodes, often brought on by very little exercise.

At this point it is probably worth giving a very brief background into what Pheochromocytoma is as none of us had ever heard of it!

Pheochromocytoma is a rare tumour of the adrenal gland tissue. It results in the release of too much epinephrine and norepinephrine hormones that control the heart rate, metabolism and blood pressure. This in turn can lead, particularly during an episode, to excess sweating, racing heart and nausea, to pick out just a few of the symptoms. If left untreated, it is extremely dangerous.

Unfortunately, it is difficult to diagnose as the tumour is extremely rare, occurring in just one in a million! Our local doctor missed it entirely and it was only by going to a private clinic and having an MRI scan that the tumour was diagnosed.

Heather was initially placed in the hands of consultants at the Royal Marsden Hospital, who decided the best hospital surgical team for this operation in London was based at Chelsea and Westminster Hospital on Fulham Road. At that time there were only three surgeons in London who had ever operated to remove this particular tumour!!

There followed a whole series of trips up to Chelsea and Westminster Hospital where further tests were carried out. By now Heather's adrenal glands were badly compromised and they calculated that her body was producing 'off the chart' adrenaline and the threat to her heart was enormous; so they had to do a course of drug therapy to reduce the adrenaline before surgery which involved several stays at the hospital. Finally the surgery was scheduled for the first week of November.

Heather was admitted and everything was geared up for her operation: first they had to stabilise her blood pressure and adrenal activity. At the time Heather was also suffering from diabetes, but in reality this was directly related to her tumour. I vividly recall a nurse running around other bedside tables collecting up Lucozade as Heather's blood sugar levels had dived. They soon came back up though. Yet another use of Lucozade!

Although our children knew that this operation was serious, I am not so sure they quite knew how serious. On the day, the whole family had lunch just down the road from the hospital, with a local orderly promising to keep me posted as to how the operation was going by phone.

Some hours later, Heather was still in the operating theatre and there was even some rather ill-advised talk in front of us of there being no beds available in the Intensive Care Department. Fortunately, there was a brilliant young doctor on Heather's old ward who promised to find out what was happening on the operating table. I heard her ripping into the appropriate senior person. Finally, Heather was out of surgery and all connected to what seemed like hundreds of pipes and equipment. I don't think any of us were totally prepared for what we saw. But Heather was alive and, considering she had been through a delicate operation lasting six hours, relatively well.

I don't think I have ever prayed so long and hard during the very long journey towards and during the operation. It later turned out that the tumour had wrapped its way around the kidneys, hence the very long operation. Better still it was benign so no need for chemotherapy and the diabetes ceased immediately with Heather's blood sugars returning to normal. Although the surgeons were brilliant, this could not be said for the aftercare.

The Intensive Care Departments' dedicated nurses switched patients every 24-hours. Although I could understand the reasons behind this, it made 'joined-up' care very difficult. There was meant to be a briefing each morning, but I usually filled in the bits they didn't know.

Heather's bed was broken, so that didn't help matters, as her legs couldn't be raised. Meals were frequently delivered without any cutlery. I was dispatched by the nurses to fetch as much cutlery from Costa Coffee next door, without getting caught. Crazy!

I remember Carrie sitting by Heather's bed, working on her essays, which I think she actually gained high marks for. Heather was unconscious for most of this week, but finally she was moved to the High Dependency Ward where nurses seemed to be at one long meeting preventing them from administrating even basic care.

While food did come with cutlery, it was often left out of reach of patients. Not only did I feed Heather in the evening, but what seemed like half the ward; Jamie found the same thing when he popped in at lunchtime to make sure his Mother got some food.

Heather spent three weeks on the ward. Then what I would call an old-style, Irish 'matron' appeared, informing Heather that she should get the hell out of the hospital as quickly as possible to avoid further infection, as there was C. diff on the ward. The consultant surgeon also advised us that if we could cope at home it would be best as Heather's enormous cut from the surgery (36 stitches) and her open sores from the oedema in her legs were all prime candidates for a hospital-acquired infection.

We brought her home but had to go a long way around due to traffic. We had moved a bed down to the lounge which meant Heather slept downstairs. Unfortunately, because it was a Friday, the Home Nursing Service didn't kick in until Monday. Heather started to vomit. The nurses wanted to send her back to hospital but fortunately met our doctor as they left who was having none of it, prescribing medication to stop her feeling so sick. Went to Boots to obtain the medication with the dispensary advising that the main side effect was nausea! But it worked.

Heather became stronger and after three weeks of community nursing, she managed to climb the stairs, and we were able to get the lounge ready for Christmas. In the New Year she started to slowly recover and to live her life to the full once again.

Not a great period of time for any of us, least of all Heather.

Slowly our busy house started to slow down as one by one our children left home. Suddenly it was just Heather and myself in a five bedroom detached house. Sadly, it was time to move although our memories still live on.

37 West Way

We never really intended to live by the sea, and certainly not near Worthing. We viewed many properties as we gradually made our way down the A3 corridor. At the time, in 2009 just after the banking crash, we still had a large mortgage which needed to be paid off quickly in order to preserve as much equity as we could for our pension pot!

Finally, after much searching and with a buyer already to go on Bradmore Way, we found a 'project' restoration on West Way and it fitted our requirements. A three-bedroom bungalow in need of a great deal of tender loving care. Oh yes, and a fabulous garden which Bonnie and Leo just loved (so did I!).

Barry (our builder friend) came down from his Old Coulsdon home each day and spent many months working on each room in turn. We slept on lilo beds for the first couple of weeks. In the end it looked absolutely lovely, again down to Heather's fabulous designs.

As we are almost up-to-date now, here is a very brief summary of the main events over 11 years in High Salvington!

Jamie and Laura getting married, a lovely and funny service plus a great reception at Kew Gardens.

Carrie turning up with a Jack Russell puppy called 'Dougie the Dog'. I couldn't speak for a couple of hours! Many wet patches later made us remove carpets one by one and go for wooden flooring! Bonnie and Leo slowly got used to Dougie who, in his mad dash around the house and garden, often flew through their legs!

Carrie became ill at a very damp flat in Arundel, living with us while she saved her deposit and then buying a house in nearby Littlehampton.

Our 40th Wedding Anniversary in a marquee in the garden. A beautiful occasion. Had we really been married for 40 years? Anyway, I am looking forward to the 50th!

Excellent neighbours, for once, especially Ken and Sue plus dog. Ken helped out every time when I was just too stupid to undertake a do-it-yourself task.

The lovely Dennis and Mrs 'Bucket' as all the neighbours called her. A heart of gold if somewhat on occasions a slight nuisance, bless her. If you didn't put your bin out on the prescribed day, she would do it for you and put it back unless you were out on the road within five minutes of the dustbin lorry leaving.

The very rapid decline in Bonnie and Leo's health. We knew they were both slowing down, but the end was sudden. First, Leo could only just about wag his tail when I came back from Portugal. On reflection, I think Bonnie missed Leo as she died in her sleep just a couple of months later. Both are very sadly missed.

I think it was safe to say that Heather never really felt at home in West Way.

Heather was, unfortunately, Chair of Governors at Lodge School and had to manage the impending bankruptcy and fallout which happened during the first year we moved; not a very good start. Heather spent many hours, days and months managing the fallout, making teachers redundant and dealing with the subsequent sale to an Education Trust. She had to deal with a very negative local press and received absolutely no support from her local church, where Heather and David had been active members for many years.

I remember we reaffirmed our vows at the church. I think Heather quickly found who her real friends were; really being Chairman should have been a hobby!

During the first few years Heather drove up to Fetcham on a Thursday and Fridays for a bit of nana day care, while Dawn was teaching.

Waking up one morning to find 10 Brighton flags planted up our front garden path having been put there the previous night by yet another neighbour, John. You guessed it, an ardent Brighton supporter.

For various reasons we decided it was time to move and we went searching for somewhere more rural away from road pollution. We fell in love with our beautiful lodge at the Royal Oak Country Park in Wineham, which gives us mortgage-free living at long last! After 15 stressful months, we finally managed to move in August 2019 , and the rest is history in the making ...

I look forward to our new life there with our lovely new Portuguese rescue dog, Bertie.

The Croydon Stagers

I grew up with the theatre in my blood. This was to a large extent influenced by my Mother's love of the Croydon Stagers and all things theatrical.

The Stagers were founded in 1908 and my Mother joined in the early 1920s. Some say she was a founding member because she had been there for longer than anyone could remember. She was secretary and so much more for 25 years.

I remember being taken along to many shows as a very young toddler and being totally in awe of the lights, music and, occasionally, the performances. Nothing put me off the stage. I would as a callow youth go on to perform in many musicals and even starred in a few – but that is another story!

Many committee meetings took place at Number 9. My Mother used to make 'Melting Moments', which contained soft oatmeal and a cherry in the middle, which usually went down a bomb with the committee on the night. Sometimes I was allowed to take them into the meeting, but there were usually a few cherries missing; they must have fallen off on my way in!

You couldn't hear what was going on, except my Mother's voice tended to monopolise the meeting. She did work very hard and was the lifeblood of the Society for many years.

My Mother, Bertie and my Father to a lesser extent were all involved throughout my childhood. It therefore seemed a natural progression for me to become involved from an early age.

I recall helping unload the costumes from the costumiers, usually Charles Fox of London, sorting them out into individual named characters and then transporting them to the appropriate dressing room. Although our Wardrobe Mistress sent individual measurements to the costumiers weeks before a show, they rarely fitted! The costumes only arrived 24 hours before the opening night.

For one show, I was very proud to be given the task of putting together a suit of armour, which was to stand on stage in one particular scene from 'Me and My Girl'. I managed to fit everything together in the correct order, except for one bit that stuck out more than anything else! I remember asking where this piece of equipment fitted and wondered why everyone was in stitches laughing; I was all of 12 at the time.

In those far off days, Stagers used to perform at the old Grand Theatre, Croydon, complete with its ornate ceilings and statues. A beautiful, traditional theatre sadly long-since demolished. I remember collecting signatures around the local area and going on marches in a vain effort to stop the closure of the old theatre. It closed in 1959 and I was there! I cannot remember why, but the owner ran off with whatever funds were left, leaving the current show unable to continue.

Although my early teens might have been spent behind the scenes, I soon progressed to performing winning the title of the last guy on the left in the back row of the chorus. I think I fairly quickly progressed to being the last one on the right in the back row of the chorus! I was only 16 going on 17 at the time. I missed out on performing at the Grand Theatre, having to make do with the old and now defunct Civic Halls. We then moved to the brand-new Ashcroft Theatre, Fairfield Halls, when they opened in 1962.

This was very exciting for the Stagers and me in particular having seen the theatre being built and being the first ever person to stand on its stage!

Most of those around my age remember where they were when Kennedy was shot. I heard just before going to a rehearsal in West Croydon. Kennedy was the new shining light, not only

101

in America but also throughout most of the world. An exciting, great visionary who was about to do what we all hoped, would be great things for peace and prosperity.

This was before social media and the original bulletin just announced that he had been shot. I was on the bus going to rehearsal with the driver stopping anyone who was walking along the pavement and at bus stops for the latest news. The driver then sadly announced to all his passengers that Kennedy had died. We were all devastated, and many were weeping. Arriving at the rehearsal hall there was stunned silence, nobody could really quite believe what had happened. The director tried to continue rehearsals, but he was fighting a battle that clearly he could not win. Most of us went across to the pub, which had the radio on full blast. There was total silence. The country was stunned.

I also became a 'dancer'. The girl dancers were usually fabulous, having attended ballet, jazz and tap classes from an early age. There were usually two or three excellent male dancers, with the choreographer forced to turn to the likes of me, plus a few other guys, to make up the numbers. I may have gone from having two left feet to two right feet over a period of several years. Oh, how hard the choreographer worked on bringing us up to an acceptable level.

There was one excellent male dancer who used to take us off to one of the side rooms to practice.   He was kind and patient, which he needed to be, not only to help me master the dance steps but also to keep them in my memory – in the right order. It must have worked to some degree as there were often around six or seven different routines in any one show. Being the worst dancer often meant that I had the worst female partner who was, in turn, difficult to lift. Occasionally I had a fabulous dancer who almost flew up to the ceiling and back during a straightforward lift and I had hardly touched her!

All I can remember during my relatively brief dancing career was becoming very fit and losing weight rapidly. Oh yes and during one very strenuous routine, from the Music Man, my elasticated trousers snapped and I had to hold them up for the rest of the dance!

As far as I recall, my first major role was Charlie Cowell in the 'Music Man'. This was a small but good character part, which involved a 'forced' kiss with a very glamorous leading lady. The rehearsal finally arrived when I had to practice the kiss, fortunately with only about five of us present, but including my Mother!! I was extremely nervous anyway, but my Mother's influence made it almost impossible to 'rehearse'.

Fortunately, I was 'dragged' off by my lovely leading lady to a small adjacent room where we practiced for a considerable period of time! So long in fact that my Mother came knocking on the door clearly quite concerned!! However, during one performance, I became so involved in my character portrayal that I unintentionally split my leading lady's lip. I was mortified and so was she!! I don't think she spoke to me for the rest of the run.

One of the most enjoyable early parts was 'Stewpot' in 'South Pacific' in the early 1960s. Being part of a very large male chorus of around 30, singing 'There is nothing like a Dame' at the top of our voices is still a happy memory.

This made me think about 'breaking out' of being a dancer to perhaps playing leading parts. I remember talking to our choreographer about my ambitions. She all too readily encouraged me with a very relieved smile on her face. However, in order to play parts in musicals, you had to be able to sing!

So, I went to a singing teacher called Eric Palmer who, although retired, had played major parts in the West End. He was always encouraging and thought that my voice was tremendous. After a few visits I asked him what he really thought of my voice away from his rather showbiz encouragement, as after all, I was paying him. There was a short silence before he announced that my voice reminded him of a circular saw! Well I had asked. Actually, he was a great teacher, who always came to see each of my so-called musical performances. He invariably came backstage afterwards telling me 'darling, what a wonderful performance', before walking away then turning back to me to make a circular saw movement. I like to think that over several years, this became an 'in-joke', but was never quite sure.

Eric also had what can only be described as a very old pianist. She never took her hat or coat off, no matter what the weather. One day during one of my lessons, she suddenly announced that she didn't feel well. Within two hours she had died.

Several Stagers also took singing lessons with him, so often I waited in his hallway while another finished their lesson. On one such occasion, he invited me in to sing 'Sixteen going on Seventeen' from the Sound of Music as a duet with a girl I rather fancied at the time, but was far too shy to do anything about. I was so embarrassed, as we were both at the right age. Not sure if it was a set up or not, but later I took her to a Heath Clark Reunion Dance. Nothing really happened, as at the time I thought most girls were far superior for the likes of me.

My 'breakthrough' part was the very meaty role of Jud Fry (the nasty psycho) in 'Oklahoma', again at the Ashcroft Theatre in 1965. How do I know it was that particular year? Google it, as the programme is now in the historical files in Croydon Library! There is a picture of a very young me plus my Mother; I think my Mother's picture might have been taken several years prior to the show!?

In 1968, Stagers had their 50th anniversary, and were lucky enough to stage the amateur premier of 'My Fair Lady', which ran for two whole weeks. The Fairfield Hall management threw a very lavish aftershow party in the main foyer, which looked magical. Several Croydon pro actors came along, so it was quite a star-studded event. A London theatrical costumier had made all the costumes especially. I will long remember my Mother's Ascot hat, which she wore throughout all the performances with great pride. The designer came on the last night and was in tears as she explained that my Mother had worn the hat back to front. Looked OK to me.

I was content with singing the backing vocals to 'Wouldn't it be lovely' coincidentally with the same '16 going on 17' girl.

Other more romantic parts followed, including leads in 'Flower Drum Song' and 'Calamity Jane'. I remember Calamity rehearsals for all the wrong reasons. We were lucky to have an excellent director, who lit up a room the moment he entered. He was also a very funny guy but totally dedicated to producing a great final production.

However, at a principal rehearsal, I was playing a scene with another guy, when he suddenly said to our director that he couldn't go on and then left the room. There was a stunned silence, with me thinking 'surely I wasn't that bad, was I?'. It turned out he was an alcoholic who had somehow managed to hide bottles around the hall and having a quick drink without any of us knowing. He also appeared to be stone-cold sober. His wife (my 'Sixteen going on Seventeen' girl) was naturally in tears, as clearly she was already aware of his problems.

This was probably my first brush with alcoholism and sadly showed how someone could hide their drink and sometimes appear sober. The positives to this story are that he managed to have a successful life. His third wife just happens to be the very good dancer that I used to effortlessly lift in my former stage career!

I also 'blacked up' for the part of Abe in a show called 'Summer Song' (hardly politically correct now, but we had no black members in those days) having to sing 'Cotton Tail' with a rabbit on my lap; which at every performance peed all over me! Oh the joys of show biz!

Just before 'Calamity', I was a knight in the rock musical 'Two Gentlemen of Verona', which involved wearing real armour (including the sticking out part!). I could only just walk. I remember singing a very romantic and loving song to my leading lady, who in reality was a few months pregnant. Most nights she rushed off stage immediately after our song to be sick in a bucket! Why did my stage kisses always turn out so badly??

The most important aspect of this show was the blind date, where I met Heather, my wife of 40+ years and counting. Now if you have been reading this book in sequence you will know that during this show I met Heather for the first time. However, it's worth repeating that at every performance we had to go into the audience and dance with whoever was willing. This often proved easier said than achieved, so the cast decided to go for people they knew or were friends of friends. That's how I was 'set up' to meet Heather, who I think was in row AA/seat20. I was more than happy to dance with my soon-to-be wife! Ok, this was mentioned in a previous chapter, but worth telling again, she changed my life.

I had been on the Stagers Committee for several years, but after 'Two Gents', I was suddenly asked to be Chairman of the Dramatic Section. One of my first jobs was to take Heather around and introduce her to my new 'dramatic' friends. Heather was keen to join the group and I was going to make quite sure she did! And guess what she did! We soon became inseparable – but that is another story!

Meanwhile, I managed to improve both the standard and finances of the Stagers, which had previously been in a very sorry state so I could hardly have failed! This was all before leaving to concentrate on other things like getting married, having children, plus my job with L&G! So, my involvement with the Croydon Stagers diminished.

Heather and I went to their 100th celebration in 2008. There were still a few people we both knew but like all things, Stagers had moved on. Sadly, after all those years, they are now defunct, as amateur shows performed at professional theatres cost in the region of £100,000 to run for a week.

Darlings, I am now a director (of shows)

I have already mentioned that by chance I got into directing pantomimes and musicals at Legal & General. This was the ideal learning curve, enabling me to try out my 'ideas' to see if they worked or not.

There were several experienced Stagers (including my long-suffering choreographer) who I invited to these L&G performances to get their take on a production, knowing that they wouldn't hold back! They never did hold back which, in turn, helped me a great deal. I might not have liked what they said but, on reflection, their opinions were usually correct.

Stagers had always used professional directors, some of whom weren't that great. So, imagine my surprise when the then Stagers Chairman asked me to direct their next musical. I sputtered out, "why me?", only to be informed that I couldn't be worse than the previous pro director! I was, therefore, their very first amateur director.

I was lucky enough to be given this brilliant chance, especially as their next show was to be the amateur premier of 'Irene' which had just finished in the West End after a run of over a year. Even better we had the original scenery and costumes, all of which looked a million dollars. I could hardly fail, and I apparently didn't!

Although I was obviously unaware at the time, I would go on to direct 148 plays and musicals over the years. Please don't worry, I am not about to go through each of the 148 productions, but plan to pick out some of my most successful and proudest shows, along with a few disasters.

As well as church halls and small theatres, I directed many musicals at professional theatres, such as the Wimbledon Theatre, Kings Theatre Portsmouth, Churchill Theatre Bromley and, of course, the Ashcroft. All of these theatres naturally had professional stage managers and lighting designers, in fact the full works! They were not always that friendly towards amateurs in general and in particular amateur directors!

However, I soon learnt that if you could throw in a few technical terms and name lighting equipment for example, a 'patt 23', you were in! This guy must know what he is talking about, even though I most certainly did not!

With live performances there is always an element of surprise as, no matter how often you rehearse, the unexpected can happen. It certainly happened one night during the run of 'South Pacific' at the Wimbledon Theatre. In the 1980s Wimbledon Theatre was still in its original state with gold on the ornate ceilings, the 'Gods', where the audience just sat on wooden benches. Miles of rope where the scenery was pulled up and down by hand, the only counterweight being bags with sand in them. It also had, and still does have, an enormous raked stage so you sang and danced on a slope. For some reason it even had a Turkish bath in the basement!

However, it was the raked stage, which nearly stopped my show. 'Nellie Forbush' the lead in South Pacific had to wash her hair on stage, complete with soap and water from an on-stage shower. While washing her hair, she also had to sing, 'I'm Gonna Wash That Man Right Outa My Hair'. All went well until she left the shower on the first night but it failed to turn off! I was with the lighting designer who was watching the water slowly making its way to the front of the stage which housed a huge armour of electrics. He was just about to stop the show when, to our amazement, one by one the dancers stood fully-clothed in the running shower while the rest of the girls brought on towels from their dressing room to form a damn.

Disaster was averted in the nick of time and the full house of 1,500 people didn't really notice a thing.

Come to think of it, the same show had probably the worst orchestra I have ever had the misfortune to hear. In fact, at the dress run, the 18-piece orchestra had to play the same chord at the start of 'Some Enchanted Evening', only for the leading man to step forward at the dress rehearsal and ask which note he should pick!

June Whitfield, of 'Ab Fab' and 'Terry and June' fame, also attended on the Saturday night as she lived locally. Apparently South Pacific was her first show in the West End and, even though she was in the chorus, she could still remember every word. She sang and danced her way through several of the numbers for us backstage before the last night – absolutely fabulous – sorry! There is a section of the show, which is staged as a show-within-a-show, in which the on-stage chorus heckle the concert hall actors. June was in the front row of the dress circle. She stood up and heckled my company who gave as good as they got back to her. The audience loved it but I guess most of them must have wondered who she was as the front of house lights were down!

'Fiddler on the Roof' provided another disaster as one night Tevye's 'wife' totally missed her cue to make her entrance. She appeared to be still in her dressing room which, in turn, was some way from the stage. The actor playing Tevye turned to the audience and gave a quite brilliant off-the-cuff story of the early life of Tevye before she suddenly arrived on stage, unfortunately half-dressed. He turned to her and said something along the lines of, "you could have dressed for the occasion". This produced a standing ovation from the audience and was a great example of how lessons on 'how to ad lib' can prove to be beneficial.

There is a barbershop quartet in 'The Music Man', where all four start facing upstage and then each turns to face the audience as their singing part is introduced. This looked great in rehearsal. However, on the night they were facing a tree situated just upstage from them. The audience fell about laughing as it looked as though they were all having a pee! I quickly changed this for the rest of the run.

Ok, so that is just a small selection of 'missteps' that I encountered as a director. It can also happen in the West End!

While working for L&G in London, we had a Christmas staff outing to see the Royal Shakespeare Company's production of 'The Wizard of Oz' at one of the London theatres. A huge amount of money had been spent on this production, including going from 'black and white' to colour, just like the beginning of the film.

Their disaster started when Dorothy and her dog 'landed' in Oz. As she walked around the beautiful set, I saw fear and panic come into her eyes. The curtain came down and we were informed there would be a short break. The show had only been going for five minutes! All we could hear was crashing and banging – then the show resumed. Just like the film, the glass bubble came flying into view complete with the Wicked Witch of the West, clearly absolutely terrified after having been stuck high above the stage all that time. Dorothy even had to help her out of the 'bubble'?

Later, the Cowardly Lion's tail fell off and he rushed off stage to get it fixed. I know many amateurs who would have laughed, joked and interacted with the kids in the audience. Not this guy who just panicked. The kids had him for breakfast shouting out, "Mister, your tail's fallen off again" throughout the show; and this was the Royal Shakespeare Company!

Once, during my short-lived 'musical acting career', while I was in the middle of a number with another guy the theatre's stage sprinkler system came on. We finished the number soaking wet. I think this was the only time that I ever received a standing ovation from the audience!?

Every now and then a production comes along which just seems destined to succeed. This may be due to the show itself, the standard of the principal leads, or even the director, or perhaps a mixture of all three plus a liberal sprinkling of fairy dust!? One such show was 'Chicago', staged at the Epsom Playhouse.

The main leads were both ex-professionals and the rest of the company were not far behind them. However, in this case, the extra 'fairy dust' was provided by the Wimbledon College of Arts, whose students designed and made the costumes and set for their final exams. This, in turn, meant that I had numerous meetings with the students prior to the production.

The original final scene in Chicago was rather strange with the two leads Roxy and Velma throwing out gladiolas into the audience. I think Barry Humphries may have half-hitched the idea. So, I asked the college students to come up with an outrageous alternative idea for the final scene. Their design work for the rest of the show had already produced excellent ideas and the execution was first class.

Finally, these wonderful students revealed their outrageous ideas for a spectacular ending. The set would split open to reveal a chariot containing Roxy and Velma drawn by two working, full-size model horses which slowly moved downstage. I added white lights to initially blind the audience so the surprise was even greater as the chariot came slowly out of the dry ice to a full reveal. To say the audience loved it each night was an understatement. After the final show, the students confessed to me that they had thought of the idea five minutes before my final meeting with them!

As the examiners wanted to see the costumes and set, we took the whole show to the college which had a large stage and full lighting rig. You can imagine how every scene was greeted. Both examiners came to see me after the show. They were totally 'knocked out' by the students' work and mentioned that they had never seen such a high standard. I think they all received A* grades!

As a director, shows like 'Annie' and 'Oliver' have one major drawback. They all have a copious number of children! By law you have to have two separate sets, as children are not allowed to undertake two continuous performances. So, for 'Oliver', this meant around 40 kids in the 10–12 age group.

I have nothing against working with children, especially as when they succeed (which they usually do) during the run of any show, this gives me tremendous satisfaction.

I directed 'Oliver' at the Kings Theatre in Portsmouth, along with 40 boys mostly from the docks area. Asking them to have their right foot forward at the same time proved difficult to say the very least! I will long remember the boys entering in line at the dress rehearsal for "Food, Glorious Food" which opens the show and one-by-one they just stopped singing and their mouths dropped open. It turned out that none of them had ever been inside a theatre before.

I think I directed 'Oliver' three times – never again!

As an aside, I once played Bill Sykes in 'Oliver' at the Ashcroft Theatre! I remember this for four reasons. The set was designed in levels above the stage, the higher point being some 30 feet. That was my first entrance and I am afraid of heights! Sykes doesn't appear until just before the interval, so I spent an hour or so during Act 1 all by myself as everyone was on stage. You get kind of nervous! I had a bulldog, which was inclined to bite me if I moved too quickly.

Finally, as I made my way down to stage level, I had to 'kick' various boys out of the way. Years later, while shopping in Purley, this guy in his early twenties, came up to me, "Don't expect you remember me Bill, but you used to kick me out of the way every night!". The price of fame!

Years after directing 'Annie', I just couldn't listen to "Tomorrow" or "It's the Hard-Knock Life". You had to have two Annie's as well!

One of my most exciting shows was 'West Side Story'. A wonderful score, which you can never get bored with, plus an exciting storyline! I had the wonderful opportunity of casting both the main leads and dancers via adverts placed in The Stage newspaper.

The day of the auditions dawned, which were to be held at the Churchill Theatre in Bromley. Not knowing who, if anybody, would turn up; I was met with well over 100 young fellas and girls all ready to audition.

Some were dressed as Sharks and Jets. My attention was, however, immediately drawn towards a young girl dressed as Maria – I just hoped she could act, sing and dance as she was everyone's idea for the part. Fortunately, it turned out that she could do all three! We found a great cast and an excellent choreographer. The atmosphere was electric during rehearsals.

The set was designed by the fella who was responsible for the barricades in Les Misérables (he happened to be the next-door neighbour of someone in the cast!). The set consisted of moveable, continuous scaffolding at various heights around the very large Churchill stage. All we needed now was a fantastic orchestra to do justice to the music.

Oh, we had this in bucketfuls! As a result of the same advert in The Stage for the actors and dancers, word got around the musical fraternity. Our musical director received phone call after phone call from pro musicians, many of whom came from the BBC Symphony Orchestra and the Royal Philharmonic Orchestra pleading to be part of this orchestra. Just as actors would 'die' to take part in West Side Story, so do pro musicians just love the exciting Bernstein score.

We ran for 10 sell-out nights with the Box Office asking if they could sell seats for the dress rehearsal; and they did! I was lucky enough to have the honour of directing this show twice.

'Cabaret' is another favourite of mine. I set the show in a totally blank open stage, painted all black. I wanted to emphasise the show plunge into the Nazi influence in the lead up to the Second World War. In many ways this is a very disturbing musical play, so there is plenty of dramatic meat to get my teeth into – so to speak. This in turn meant that my version of Cabaret would rely heavily on the lighting design.

Over the years I had developed a great interest in lighting, realising you could make a good show look a million dollars with skilful lighting. Don't get me wrong, I always relied on the pro lighting director for the final design, but met up with him on several occasions to discuss my ideas as well as provide the 200 or so cues needed in shows such as 'Cabaret'.

Imagine my dismay when on the technical dress rehearsal, the day rigging of the lights were due to take place, my lighting designer went down sick. However, out of disaster came a heavenly solution. My designer mentioned that his replacement would arrive within the hour and I would like him! Well he arrived within the hour! I recall talking to him on the Churchill stage surrounded by unusually attentive pro staff. He asked me my overall concept of the show then barked out orders to everyone and the lighting rig slowly began to take shape.

I decided that unusually for a tech rehearsal, I would just let the show run uninterrupted so he could see my production (usually the lighting designer saw at least a previous rehearsal). I talked him through my ideas as the show progressed.

I arrived at the theatre the following morning at 8am as promised. The theatre was in turmoil, with pieces of lighting equipment arriving what seemed like every two minutes. I then found out why I would like him. He was Disneyland Paris' chief lighting designer! No wonder the pro guys were in awe of him!

As a result, I had a brilliant lighting design, which included six follow-spot operators, four of whom were suspended in cages from the stage producing weird effects which was just what I wanted but more! Probably one of the best lighting designs I have ever seen. The audience just gasped at some of the effects.

During rehearsals, I had the idea of the audience arriving with the curtain up and all the cast already on stage but totally still in various poses for around 15 minutes prior to the start. This took a great deal of rehearsing! However, it worked with the audience just staring at the stage (probably just waiting for anyone to move or faint!?).

But I wasn't quite finished with 'statues' – I hit on the idea of using a metronome to start the performance so that they moved just one pace on every 10th beat, then the 9th until they moved into the show properly. It always got a round of applause, but I think the company might not have been so keen during rehearsals.

Oh, by the way, I once directed the musical version of 'Paddington Bear' with the author's wife providing the funds for the production. She had some lovely stories about Michael Bond, great fun, and she got her money back.

One of the more unusual shows to direct was 'Barnum' which is, as I am sure you know, about the circus and the life and times of this showman. The film 'The Greatest Showman' has further enhanced the story.

It is unusual as the main lead (Barnum) has to learn to walk a tightrope across the stage. The guy I was lucky enough to have had previously played the part in Australia and was currently the stage doorkeeper at the Drury Lane Theatre, London where at the time 'Miss Saigon' was being staged. One Sunday I just rehearsed with 'Barnum' who had brought his girlfriend with him. It subsequently turned out that she was playing Miss Saigon. At the end of the rehearsal, I took both of them back to Bromley railway station. I enquired more in hope that in return she would sing for me. So, as we drove along, she sang a few of her songs from the show. To this day, an absolutely magical experience.

I often used to be asked what my all-time favourite and most successful show is. This is a difficult question, as it is hard to compare musicals that have such diverse music and storylines. However, up at the top of my favourites must be '42nd Street'.

The show has spectacular sets and costumes with hit songs and dance numbers throughout the musical. Because of this, superb actors who can dance and sing are essential to its success. Fortunately, we had an entire company that more than achieved these essentials in bucketfuls.

A company that, from the word go, was totally dedicated to making certain that '42nd Street' was a smash hit! As a director, it is quite fantastic and unusual to walk into a rehearsal studio where there is already a vibrant atmosphere. Too often I have had to struggle half the evening to get things up and running. But not for this show.

We were to run '42nd Street' for two whole weeks at the Churchill Theatre plus, of course, a technical rehearsal and a dress rehearsal!

This was one show that I just couldn't wait for the two-week run to start. In fact, I actually had to push back on the company's enthusiasm just to make sure they would peak at the right time. A little like a football manager preparing his team for an important match, I guess – maybe?

However, everything was perfect until the 'get in' when the scenery normally arrives via a huge lorry, usually at 8am in the morning. Except it didn't! Fortunately, the pro staff knew the driver's mobile number. He had fallen asleep at his overnight stop! This meant he would be around five hours late. We were due to start the tech rehearsal at 7.30pm!

Fortunately, I knew a stage manager who had previously done the show, knew the scenery and, more importantly, how to put the trucks together and 'fly' the rest of the scenery in its correct order. One phone call later, he arrived at the theatre just before the lorry. He literally saved the tech, as he immediately took over and everything was up-and-ready to go by the 7.30pm kick off. The pro staff even gave up their lunch and tea breaks, which was extremely unusual!

Each set looks a million dollars but involves a great deal of very quick changes. We staggered through until early in the second act when the whole show finally collapsed. The pro stage manager had erected the wrong set in the wrong place! It was the only time, in 148 shows, when I have seen a pro stage manager cry and at the same time apologising over and over again.

We called it a night, after all it was nearly midnight anyway!

However, my company was still totally almost swinging from the rafters, so there was absolutely no need for a motivational talk from me.

I have previously mentioned that lighting a show had become very important to me. The show screamed for a brilliant lighting design to accentuate the dancer's fab costumes, not to mention the sets plus some fairy dust in the form of showbiz razzle-dazzle.

There were over 300 lighting cues, which I sat for hours imagining and designing. That, in turn, meant 300 separate complete designs to be manually worked through and then computerised.

The pro lighting designer had already seen several rehearsals and promised to work through the night to rig the lighting (he owed me as it was the same guy who had got sick before 'Cabaret'!).

I remember arriving at the theatre at 8am the following morning and working non-stop with him until five minutes before the dress rehearsal scheduled for 7.30pm.

We had a complete sell-out fortnight, which always helps the atmosphere, but I was totally unprepared for what was about to happen on the opening night. This may have been because I was by this time swaying in the breeze, having not only completed the lighting set, but gone through all the sound mic cues. I think there were some 20 radio mics plus general sound that picked up the tap dances and helped balance orchestra with soloists etc. The show begins with what was an excellent band playing the start of the '42nd Street' number with the curtain slowly rising about 3ft, to reveal some 20 girl dancers undertaking a full tap routine in a straight line across the front of the stage, with just cross lighting on their feet and legs.

I have never seen a whole audience rise to their feet as one for an opening number; and they kept doing this for every number that followed and there were plenty of them!

I sat there almost totally detached from what was going on, trying to concentrate on what could be improved for the following night, especially lighting and sound wise. I looked around towards the sound and lighting boxes situated at the rear of the theatre and they all seemed to be concentrating and working seamlessly. Perhaps it was just a dream?

At the end of the show, I lost count of the number of curtain calls and standing ovations, before the stage manager decided to call it a night.

Often when I go backstage at the end of any show, I have to lie just a little, saying, "lovely show everyone" when sometimes it was anything but. This time, however, I could be totally honest. Usually I find everyone back in their dressing rooms, but not this time. The company was mostly on the floor of the stage or hugging each other. Everyone was crying, and that was just the men!

No one had ever experienced anything quite like the reception they had just received. I remember saying, "don't cry, it was bloody brilliant", only to find that I was in tears (probably through fatigue). I went to thank all the pro staff for working so hard on this show. You normally find them in the bar but they hadn't made it; I discovered them sitting in a corridor leading to the bar with just the hint of a tear in their eyes. Most of them had been working through the previous night, so again it must have been fatigue!

Occasionally when a particular musical is successful, after a couple of nights into the run I have a rather strange reaction. The show 'grows' as performance, lighting etc. become slicker. I suddenly feel that I had nothing to do with the production whatsoever. But that is just me – weird!

'42nd Street' will long live in my memory for a very different reason. During the run, my Mother died. She had been in a home for a number of years and had reached the stage where she no longer recognised her family. I received a call from the matron of her home asking me to come very quickly, as she was about to pass away. As I arrived, the matron met me and prepared me for what I might find. I found a 'Mummy' who not only recognised me but also was anxious to hear all my news. This included all the latest about her grandchildren. She was delighted to hear that '42nd Street' was such a success. She remembered all the parts she had ever played.

In other words, I had my Mother back for about 15 minutes. Then she closed her eyes and I said goodbye and I went to leave her room. The matron said I should wait for five minutes as she would probably pass away in those few moments, and she did. Apparently, this happens once in about 500 cases, is known by doctors but is rarely spoken about or acknowledged.

In a way that was an uplifting a part of my life to once again reconnect with my Mother, if only for a very short space of time.

So, in conclusion, what did I learn from all those shows?

A few of my 'stars' went on to become successful West End performers. A couple combined their professional acting career with amateur performances. Nick Owen who I worked with at the Miller Centre, Caterham went on to read the ITV news for many years.

I guess the only one who became a household name was Nigel Harman who played both 'Oliver' and then 'Artful Dodger' for me at the Wimbledon Theatre. Nigel went on to play Dennis Rickman in EastEnders followed by a very successful career on the West End stage. He is currently on the pro directing circuit. However others found out the hard way that, assuming they were lucky enough to actually get a professional gig, they often hated their role and that it was easier to gain parts they enjoyed on the amateur circuit along with a 'proper' job.

What did I learn?

How to 'control' and motivate a chorus of singers and dancers, often around 40–50 diverse characters, and teach them a routine but still provide an enjoyable experience a couple of times a week.

How to gain the very best out of my principals who, after all, to a larger extent would guarantee the success or otherwise of each show.

I therefore learnt a great deal on how to deal with each of them; if one required a 'push' every now and then because they were either overconfident, thought they were better than they actually were or just plain lazy. Most needed a boost to their self-esteem so required a smile and constant encouragement. The majority were a joy to work with but there was always the occasional exception where things did not go well. Heather and I usually left the theatre as quickly as possible on the 'final Saturday night'.

Sometimes there were tears of frustration from one of the principals, but this was usually because they knew they could do better or couldn't quite reach that top A musical note. You also learn that some people, sometimes those who you least expect can be very vulnerable and fragile.

Occasionally I had a difference of opinion with the musical director or the props department but it was rare in the scheme of things.

Like most shows, the real work is done before the first rehearsal, as many hours are spent on deciding my particular 'spin' on the musical. For example, whether I wanted to make it as spectacular as possible, concentrate on the large dance routines or make it all about the principals. So most of the 'blocking' of the principal moves, plus at least a few of the chorus routines, are mapped out well before the first rehearsal.

I often used to work on a particular number during my L&G lunch breaks. Very occasionally, I had 'writers block', when I couldn't think of a single move! Panic took over sometimes even while driving to rehearsal. Fortunately I had Heather, who was well into drama and all things stage-related. She was a qualified speech and drama teacher previously and a very talented amateur actress when she had time to indulge. She was, therefore, very supportive when I swanned off to rehearsals two or three times a week. Heather also had a great talent for bringing me back down to earth and reminding me of the real world. I was, however, aware that she was coping with a growing family, while I tripped the 'light fantastic'.

Thank you Heather, for all your patience and understanding, I really do appreciate your loving and caring nature.

Although I was on the amateur directing circuit, I always received a fee for each production. So, Heather and I always made sure that we used the funds to purchase a particular piece of furniture or for a lovely holiday.

I like to think that my so-called 'talents' also helped me to further my L&G career, not to mention Learning Performance.

Not many people are lucky enough to have such a satisfying hobby that also pays (although not that well!).

9 The Close

Brancaster Lane

4 The Close

Bradmore Way

West Way

Fairfields

Rose and Ted Starbuck

Me aged 3

My Grandparents Herbert and Emily Dykes

Heather and Roger on the beach

Learning Performance

During one of the many occasions L&G made or threatened to make selective staff redundant, I fell into the dispensable category during the early 1990s. In fact, at one stage, I appeared to be right at the top of their list, as the first department to be axed always seems to be training.

I clearly remember being on one of our lovely Center Parcs holidays when Heather noticed a very small advert in the national press for a 'Franchise Opportunity in Education'. Heather immediately bombed off to the phone kiosk (it was long before mobile phones!) to register our interest, plus of course find out what was involved.

As a result, we subsequently met up with John Dibley the Australian franchisor owner and his wife in a posh London hotel for an interview. By this time we were really excited about this franchise opportunity so we were suitably gutted when we were rejected! However, a few days later we received a phone call from John asking if we were still interested. Well you bet we were interested! Apparently, the so-called 'successful applicants' had reconsidered and had turned down the opportunity – idiots. This franchise really suited our skill sets, Heather was passionate about study skills as she was using many of the techniques with her dyslexic students and felt that all students would benefit from knowing how to study effectively. With the threat of redundancy forever in our minds, it also meant we might be able to create a business for ourselves and become self-employed.

So in 1992 we, or rather Heather, started the task of setting up Learning Performance Seminars (UK) Ltd as it was then called. Heather and I attended a four-day London workshop for GCSE/A Level students, which John presented while we watched and took copious notes. That was our training done! Later that summer we each presented our first four-day workshops!! For the next few years we ran a series of these workshops at King's College, London during the summer holidays. That was it really, except that every year we added more dates so that in the end the London workshops ran weekly for six weeks. Other venues were added and after six years we had around 12 university venues across the UK all offering the four-day residential holiday courses! All from adverts placed in the national press from which the bookings from parents just poured in.

I vividly remember the day Princess Diana died in a car crash.

I had just started driving to King's College for a weekend daily workshop for the under-11s. Luckily, there were many parents present as I was not sure how I could have handled the day if they hadn't been around. I had the car radio tuned to Capital which was playing very quiet reflective music, with a very emotional presenter announcing her death every five minutes. The only other thing I remember on the drive up was that every single flower shop was open. Otherwise, like everyone else, I was completely stunned.

I decided to hold a one-minute silence in respect and then carried on as though nothing had happened. My acting skills came to my rescue. At lunchtime a few of the mothers present said that they were going to take their children down the road to Kensington Palace. We rounded up a few other children and headed off.

We were one of the very first to place flowers; this would very soon become a carpet of flowers. Suddenly, we were surrounded by photographers. One of the mothers yelled at them to stop taking photos. I am unsure if this would happen today but all the photographers put down their cameras and stood back until the children had paid their respects.

A very sad time for the entire country.

As you can imagine, Heather and I worked very hard during the summer months. I was still working for L&G, so I recruited a couple of their excellent presenters to help us out. Oh yes and recruited Nikki Dingle, our next-door neighbour, in a chance encounter over the fence one Sunday morning.

We started the business in the little bedroom at 4 The Close, moved to the study/office at Bradmore Way, onwards and upwards to the conservatory followed rapidly in 2000 to our first 'shed' office in the garden. That was before garden offices became popular.

I was keen for L&G to make me redundant, but they were not so obliging and in the end I just had to hand in a month's notice and walk away! Best thing I ever did as it was so exciting seeing Learning Performance grow!

Heather was keen to market the techniques to schools, she had been working at Thomas More School and managed to persuade the headteacher to let us practice on his students! It was all happening. Heather rewrote the four-day programme so that it fitted nicely into the average school day. Her work and dyslexia qualification proved invaluable.

This transition from back bedroom to office space shows how quickly the business expanded. I nearly forgot, we added an extension to the back of our garden office to accommodate desk space for Nick, me, Heather and two admin assistants, all this was quickly followed by a satellite rented office in the local business park, to cope with sales orders and accounts. This is where I later clearly saw a ghost, with our girls always being aware of a friendly presence – weird.

Enough of that, in 2004 we purchased Cricket View in Caterham. We had our very own new three-story office; it was ours and the Building Society's! By the end of the first decade, Learning Performance had nine staff excluding ourselves. Heather worked her socks off. We even had one girl working most evenings in the garden office, booking hotels for our presenters, leaving at the bewitching hour of midnight.

The main turning point for Learning Performance was Tony Blair shouting "Education, Education, Education", so for the very first time schools had the funds to invite us in. Tony turned out to be our main marketing guy! Suddenly what seemed like nearly every secondary school in the land wanted us to visit.

Heather had for some time been visiting schools to run one-day workshops. In the second year of trading Heather had a phone call from a headteacher who mentioned that one of his students had returned from their summer holidays a changed person after being on one of our courses. The headteacher wanted all his students to have our exciting strategies.

It sort of all went from there really. Every year our turnover increased by at least 100% until some 10 years later we exceeded the £1m mark.

Such a rapid expansion comes at a price. We were working in the garden 'shed' often from 8am to 6pm, then having dinner and going back to work. This was in the days before emails, so every call from either a parent or school was by phone.

It shows how quickly telephone technology advances, that a workman had to dig a trench from our house to our new office 'shed', so that a phone line could be installed. Yes, it was just prior to the digital age and we ended up with five separate phone lines in the end. Business was so good that our phones hardly stopped ringing. The downside, if there was one, was that we all had to wait until the evening before sorting out and actioning all the phone messages.

It may sound crazy, but I didn't join Learning Performance full time until February 1998, having finally decided to leave L&G. My feet never really touched the ground, as Heather immediately sent me off on a whirlwind of school presentations around the UK from Monday to Friday for, what seemed to me, week after week. I didn't really mind as I was by then in my element, although I never slept that well at the hotel night stops, so I often relied on bags of adrenalin.

Most of my school visits are now a complete blur as schools ranged from the posh private to the worst inner-city school, often in the same week. I do, however, remember a couple of outstanding moments.

I visited a private girls' school who were allowed, for one day only, to wear their own clothes. Believe it or not, they all had colour-coordinated their clothes with the colour of their Learning Performance manual cover.

In contrast, I turned up at one inner-city school, where the students were standing on their desks and I hadn't even started! In my eyes, the day was a complete disaster, but the teacher in charge was delighted; apparently they had been extremely well behaved compared to normal. Well that was all right then.

I loved visiting Liverpool schools, as the students just said what they thought. "How much do you get paid?", was a frequent question, along with, "Can I look after your watch for you mister?".

Newcastle was another delight. I was due to present at one school for two consecutive days. Several girls in year 11 offered to take me out on the town and give me a good time! The teacher warned me not to take them up on their kind offer; as if I would.

Soon I became more administrative based, although still visited schools.

We had begun to advertise for proven presenters, interviewing and then training them prior to sending them out into the big wide world of education. At the height of our business, I recall us having around 70 active presenters. We had a cross-section ranging from ex-teachers (who often were not that successful) through to mostly out-of-work actors. They were the best, knowing how to 'work a room' and detect a change of atmosphere in the classroom. This is a posh way of saying knowing immediately when they were losing the interest of the majority of the class.

Heather and I sometimes presented at the same school, often I guess on a Saturday?

I vividly remember visiting one school and teaching memory techniques. Students had to learn a series of key words by inventing a story, which could be as bizarre or colourful as they wanted.

From the very back of class, this young lad of around 15 years of age, put his hand up to volunteer to tell the class his story. I suddenly became aware that this was something quite special as there was an immediate silence from the rest of the class. He told us one of the best stories I think I had ever heard. The class rose as one and applauded him while the teacher sitting in the class gave an audible gasp and ran from the room.

I called a quick break and quietly asked one of the students at the front what had just happened. Apparently, this was the very first time this student had ever answered a question, let alone stood up and told us his story. Shortly afterwards the teacher returned with the headteacher and asked him to repeat his story.

The student was in the current GCSE year, so he hadn't said anything for five years! I hadn't done anything special but somehow the memory techniques had set free this extremely talented young lad. I liked to think he went on to do great things – hopefully.

Back to the rapid growth of Learning Performance. Things had expanded so fast that I had fallen behind (I had not actually ever started) that years' accounts. Some poor guy from our Accountant's office spent day after day going through every single invoice. Even then it probably wasn't that accurate!

We had a very early visit from HM Revenue and Customs. This was always a terrifying event, but at the time I completed each quarterly VAT return without really knowing what I was doing. There were two VAT inspectors who spent the entire morning going through our files. Heather and I were then called into the conservatory and informed that we owed her Majesty around £2.25! The older inspector was not in a joking mood and went on to inform us we could be heavily fined. However, the slightly younger inspector, then enquired if he should fetch the service revolver from their car, which quickly broke the sombre mood. Very few subsequent inspectors had a sense of humour. The joys of being self-employed.

Later Nick joined us on the sales side, he masterminded the move to Cricket View before leaving to start his own "Business for Breakfast" franchise.

David joined us when he moved down from Aberdeen, he rewrote and improved many of the workshops and added to our portfolio of programmes before going off to teach full-time at

Tiffin School in Kingston, gaining promotion within the teacher's profession.

To be honest, much of the time was just a blur of activities. We had great administrators however, in 2002, we did appoint an operations director. Although she was a great organiser of her admin staff, later she was to become a distinct problem.

Carrie also worked with Learning Performance during her school and university summer holidays.

In 2008, we both stepped back allowing our Operations Director to run the business reporting to us on a quarterly basis. Sadly, I took my eye off the ball. She was to run the business almost into the ground after saying she would like to buy us out. When we discovered the true extent of the accounts 'mismanagement', we fired her and she left the building almost immediately.

By this time it was October 2011 and Heather and I were living in West Way. We started commuting up the M23 to Caterham on a daily basis in an attempt to save the Company. Sadly, we had to make our lovely staff redundant (plus sell the office in Caterham), many of whom had been with us for years. To say the very least, it was not a happy time.

Heather and I were faced with picking up the pieces. The extent of the financial situation became even more dire once we uncovered the worst of her mess.

Fortunately, we had what turned out to be a very supportive RBS bank manager who had faith in our business. It didn't stop him ringing us every day to request how much business we had sold and, more importantly, how many cheques had come in from our schools (in those days most schools paid our invoices by cheque – a few still do to this day!).

Carrie joined us once again, first part-time and very quickly full-time. Although we kept on one super-efficient girl, paying her a huge salary to keep her on board, it was just the three of us plus Heather mainly working from home. We managed somehow, but the commute to Caterham and back was starting to kill us.

Once again Heather solved the problem, she found this really quirky office within a farm complex very near West Way at Findon. We moved (!) then found some excellent office staff and started to improve the business, led by Carrie.

I stepped back again and started my second retirement and later Carrie moved her excellent team to some great office space in Arundel.

It then became increasingly clear that education funding had virtually dried up. We still had some core business, but clearly we needed to find new markets. So, our new Partnership Scheme was born.

Later, Carrie found it increasingly difficult to carry on, so decided to step back and travel around Europe in 'Peggy', her new campervan.

My second 'retirement' was over. Heather and I were very tempted to close the business down but decided to give it another year or so, as this company was to become our pension pot it was worth keeping it for as long as possible.

Fortunately, we still had an excellent small team. A large increase in their salaries, plus extra responsibilities proved to be the way forward. I mostly worked remotely, which was possible, even in Portugal. This worked extremely well and I even managed to increase the yearly income.

Out of the blue, Nick emailed me to say that he had seen a guy on Facebook looking to buy an education company. The rest is history. Carrie and I even met the potential buyer at the Atlantico Restaurant in Salema as, believe it or not, he owned a villa nearby. We finally sold Learning Performance to him. We informed our staff in July 2019 and left the building after introducing the new owner.

It was an extremely weird experience. Saying goodbye to our staff, the business and 27 years of Learning Performance in just a few minutes was, to put it mildly, difficult. I still miss the business sometimes, but it really was the correct decision for Heather and myself. It is, after all, an extra pension nest for our long-overdue retirement.

Eight months later Covid 19 struck and all the schools were closed from 23rd March 2020. At the time of writing, it is too early to predict whether our lovely company will survive. We will have to wait to see if we ever receive all the funds from the sale …

Palace – South London and Proud!

I have already explained in a previous chapter my introduction to this wonderful, infuriating and occasionally brilliant club, which all began during my teenage years.

After the fateful Millwall match, which I went to with my Father, I always tried to attend when I could ... but never missed the really important games.

Through Stagers, and in particular the male 'dancing' troupe, I met John Heffer who was I think the only other straight guy 'in the valley' and a Palace fan. He was also the very proud owner of a brand-new bubble car, which you entered via the front. Its three wheels took us to many matches and was extremely easy to park. The two of us just lifted the car up and dropped it into a parking space! Later we gained a third passenger, John's girlfriend. She used to lie across the back parcel shelf as we sped along to the Holmesdale Stand.

I don't think Health and Safety even existed in those far off days, and it was certainly well before seat belts.

Later through Stagers I met a very zany and energetic young lady who was also, of course, an ardent Palace supporter. We used to stand on the terraces where the Arthur Wait Stand now resides. There were even grass banks at the rear of the terraces. However, Rosemary had a secret weapon, a large ship's bell attached to a thick rope which she used to wrap around the crash barriers just by the halfway line. The bell used to ring out 'loud and proud' when we scored or slowly tolled when all was not well. Needless to say, no one ever stood within twenty yards of us! She finally went off to train to become a speech therapist and I never saw her or the bell ever again.

Other early recollections include standing in a long line, usually in the rain, to do a half-time wee. You did not escape the rain even in the toilets as there wasn't a roof!

If there was a large crowd, the younger children were passed over everyone's heads to the front where they could actually see the game. In those days no one thought twice about this, it just sort of happened.

In the early sixties, we were lucky enough to have the then famous manager called Arthur Rowe who invented the 'push-and-run' style of play. Palace played some brilliant football under his guidance.

I was also lucky enough to watch Johnny Byrne play for Palace during the late 1950s and early '60s. He was probably the equivalent of today's Zaha. He was nicknamed 'Budgie' because he never stopped talking throughout an entire match. He was the only ever player to be selected for England while we were still in Division 3 (South).

I remember beating Accrington Stanley 9–0 and Barrow 8–0 all in the space of a few short weeks. Budgie scored a wonder goal beating around seven (or was it eight!) players before firing the ball past the keeper. I think this was the only occasion I can remember where the opposition players actually applauded his goal.

What a time to fall in love with Palace.

Then, to cap it all, along came Real Madrid to Selhurst Park – yes, really! It was 1962 and Palace had installed new floodlights (rather than candles!) and wanted to mark the occasion. Someone had the bright idea of inviting Real Madrid and to everyone's astonishment they came. At the time foreign clubs hardly ever visited the UK, so this was an amazing scoop, particularly as they were then in the middle of winning the European cup five years in a row.

I paid 30 shillings to attend, which was a large amount of money some 60-odd years ago. However, it certainly didn't put people off attending, as there was a crowd of some 25,000 at the game.

Byrne had just been sold to West Ham but was allowed to come back for this one special game! We saw these Spanish legends for the first time in the flesh rather than on a flickering black and white TV. The likes of Di Stéfano, Gento and Puskás to name but a few.

You tend to remember odd things about the match, like the Spanish players coming out holding bouquets of flowers which in turn they tossed into the crowd. We had never seen anything like this before. The rain poured down for the entire match, but I never even noticed that I was soaked to the skin. The Spanish players hardly seemed to look up when they had the ball, knowing exactly where their teammates were. The football played appeared to be silky and smooth, with the crowd often gasping in amazement at their approach play.

Palace was 4-1 down at half-time, but no one really was that worried. This was after all an exhibition match, although no one seemed to have informed the Palace players. I will long remember Byrne gathering the entire team around him. The result was an explosive second half. We just charged at them, which I rather doubt the Spanish players had ever experienced before.

We lost 4-3, but for the final 20 minutes, Real Madrid was under siege. Well I like to think they were anyway. I know they resorted to fouling everyone and then rolling around in mock agony every time we touched them.

A night to remember.

Cliff Holton was an early hero of mine. I think Palace was the wrong end of the table but recall his first game for a number of reasons. It was Boxing Day 1963, icy cold and starting to snow as the match progressed. Cliff was something special, having played 198 times for Arsenal before making his way to us via Watford and Northampton Town. He was one of those few players who could galvanise the whole team around him. Plus, he had a fantastic shot rivalling Bobby Charlton. The ball used to scorch into the net with the goalie hardly moving. He would stay with us for 101 games scoring 40 goals. However, he would have to wait a while as that Boxing Day game was the last football match until March; this was the famous freezing winter of 1963 with over six foot of snow and no underground heating in those days for the playing surface.

I saw some great players and a few disasters during the 1960s to the 1980s.

John Jackson, our goalie (we almost always seemed to recruit excellent goalkeepers), who played from 1964 to 1973 notching up 346 appearances.

This included our first ever promotion to the topflight, which happened (you can tell I have Googled this!) in 1969. Steve Kember who came up through the ranks scored the winner. I remember running onto the pitch along with almost the entire crowd and dancing and singing for what seemed like hours. I don't think there were any stewards? Steve first played for us when he was just 17 and was an instant success. There was a very strange incident involving Kember during one game. He shot into the side netting, but to most of us in the crowd plus the referee it looked like a goal. In fact, the referee gave a goal (pre-VAR days!) only for Kember to confess that actually it wasn't. Such honesty was rare, even then but I think our manager went ballistic at him.

Kember was still involved in the Club having come back as caretaker manager for just two games including the famous Stockport game in 2001. I think we can all remember where we were that day! Those of us who are Palace supporters certainly can!

Players, especially those who were really dedicated to the Club, tended to stay for many years.

Mel Blyth played Centre Back in 216 games for us during 1968–74.

Jim Cannon, yet another Centre Back, played even longer for us; in fact some 571 appearances between 1973–1988, wow! I can remember him now, usually covered in mud with a cut above his eye, head swathed in bandages and that was before the game even kicked off!

There were many more but I cannot resist mentioning Nigel Martyn, who turned out for 272 games during 1989–1996. He was the first £1 million goalie and we sold him for a profit.

The other huge character was of course, Malcolm Allison (Big Mal) who was our manager from 1973–1976 and then again in the early 1980s. Big Mal presided over a real rollercoaster of a ride.

He rebranded the Club from the Glaziers to the Eagles, plus introduced the famous red and blue strip. Jim Cannon summed it up perfectly when he said, "he was the only manager to take us from Division One to the 3rd tier in two seasons and still be an instant hero".

He also took us on the famous FA Cup run to the semi-finals during 1975–76 when we beat Leeds, Chelsea and Sunderland before losing out to Southampton who went on to win the Cup.

Big Mal became even more of a celebrity during this run with his Fedora hat and cigar becoming his trademarks. Despite his larger-than-life personality, he was one of the first to introduce the sweeper system, although I don't think we quite mastered his methods.

Allison often made the front pages of The Sun, being involved with Christine Keeler and the Profumo Scandal. After one Palace match, the players heard him coming down the corridor with yet another girl. Apparently, they leapt out of the bath as Big Mal entered with Fiona Fullerton (a Bond star). Both immediately took off their clothes except for the Fedora hat and cigar and posed for pictures in the players' bath.

I cannot resist one further story when he became the Manchester City manager. City beat Man United 4–1 and not only did he walk around their ground with four fingers raised but hired a steeplejack to lower their flag to half-mast.

Above all, he was a great football innovator and changed Palace forever.

That is about it as far as the Palace story goes. A young Jamie and Richie joined the family supporter lounge, followed by the Sainsbury's End, Lower Holmesdale and finally the Upper Holmesdale. Also, Carrie joined us during the later years.

We can all remember Ian Wright and company. Andy Johnson and, of course, Speroni yet another brilliant goalie who almost single-handedly saved us from relegation from the top flight – several times!

The highs and lows plus seven years in the Premier League. Long may it continue … South London and Proud!

The Starbuck Ancestry Line

As many of my readers will know, I have spent hours, days, weeks and even years researching our Family Tree! Much of this work was done via Ancestry.co.uk, but also by contacting various councils who often, for a fee, will look up old handwritten church records, especially those from the 16th and 17th century and earlier. Occasionally I have attempted to explain my exciting discoveries but have almost immediately found a glazed expression comes over everyone's eyes.

So, here is a quick look at the more interesting bits.

Some say the name Starbuck comes from the village of Starbeck in Yorkshire, formally spelt 'Starbuk'. This spelling appears in the 1086 Domesday Book indicating a Norse/Viking origin.

Some years ago, I attended an Ancestry Exhibition where I had a DNA swab taken. I therefore automatically entered their database. Any other Starbucks can check to see if they have the exact same or very similar DNA.

More about this later.

My DNA history showed that my ancestors had travelled through most of the world but there was a definite link to Vikings. They were known for pillaging and doing lots of unmentionable things to young women across Europe before then calling on their wives to join them!

More recent revelations confirm my ancestors, the Vikings, were often as 'high as a kite!'. Their particular drug was 'stinking nightshade' which led to a flushed face, hyperactivity and a tendency to strip naked.

There are several derivations of the name Starbuck but on our strand during the 15/16th century it is shown as Starbuck(e).

For some reason, our branch of the Starbucks moved south to Barnet before upping sticks to the seaside of Brighton and Hove, but this didn't take place until the 19th century. I suspect because there was more work down in the South of England.

I would have liked to find that in the past we were related to aristocracy or wealth at the very least, but this was not the case. We mostly worked on the land but certain appeared not to possess any form of wealth whatsoever!

I found one couple, Daniel and Elizabeth in the 1600s who had eight children, including a Roger and a Jamie. However, to cut a very long story short, I finally discovered Edward who was born in 1584 and his wife Ann, who he married on the 8th May 1603 at St Nicholas Church, Nottingham.

They subsequently had four children, Edward (1604), Margene (1606), William (1607) and Elizabeth (1608). Edward, as you have probably already guessed, is the famous son who went to New Hampshire, and William is the boring one who is our direct descendent. William married Elizabeth Bennett on 12th June 1636 in Rathbourne, Derbyshire and the rest is history.

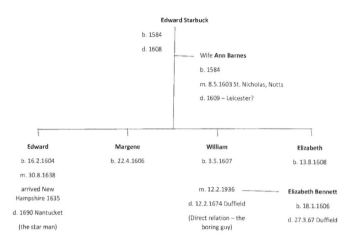

Edward Starbuck

b. 1584

d. 1608

Wife **Ann Barnes**

b. 1584

m. 8.5.1603 St. Nicholas, Notts

d. 1609 – Leicester?

Edward	Margene	William	Elizabeth
b. 16.2.1604	b. 22.4.1606	b. 3.5.1607	b. 13.8.1608
m. 30.8.1638			
arrived New Hampshire 1635		m. 12.2.1936 ·········	**Elizabeth Bennett**
d. 1690 Nantucket		d. 12.2.1674 Duffield	b. 18.1.1606
(the star man)		(Direct relation – the boring guy)	d. 27.3.67 Duffield

Edward Starbuck (the 'star man' of the Starbuck dynasty) who was born in 1604 was the guy who subsequently left the UK in 1635, later becoming one the founding fathers of the Massachusetts Bay Colonies and Nantucket Island to name but a few. Edward then went on to make his fortune in the whaling industry. In other words, he was our star man!

I was therefore keen to find out if we were directly related.

It started to look promising as many of our ancestors prior to the last century, were born and lived in the Derbyshire or Nottinghamshire areas. Edward having been born in Draycott, Derby.

I met a number of other Starbucks online, who also helped me trace some of the more obscure family members including a lady who specialises in the various Starbuck family trees throughout the world. Although she found my tree fascinating, there was a potential weak link in the chain … Daniel, the son of William (the boring one) was not born until Edward was into his 40s, which was rather unusual for that time. So, there could have been another son, with a different wife. However, we would never know as these records were all destroyed in a fire a few years ago.

Stay with me, as more exciting news later!

Edward and Ann (the parents of our boring William plus the 'star' Edward and two daughters), both sadly died within a year of each other in 1608 and 1609, when their children were very young.

At the time, there was a small plague, plus very little food to eat. We will, I fear, never know who brought up their family. There is little hope of going back further than Edward and Ann, who were born in 1584, as the only records were kept by the Lords and Dukes, who owned much of the land, whom they both probably worked for. Occasionally, servants are mentioned in Wills, but I suspect that sort of research will have to wait for several rainy days with nothing else to do. So, in the end, there was nothing very remarkable on the Starbucks tree.

I do however remember my father going off to meet other male Starbucks, for a reunion someone had organised I think at the service station on the M1 during the early 1960s.

There was a photo taken and I recall thinking how their faces and bone structures were all so similar. Much later, when Heather and I were clearing out 9 The Close, we could frustratingly find no trace of the photo or who organised the 'reunion'.

Ah yes, back finally to my DNA!

Last year (2019), I suddenly had an email from an American Starbuck who had exactly the same DNA as myself! Suddenly, the Starbuck Family Tree was complete. The American guy went way back in time and was directly related to Edward, who was the brother of William (our boring direct ancestor) – yessss! So my tree was authenticated via this DNA match!

We do also have a family crest, so perhaps after all, we are famous?

Sometime soon Heather and I plan to visit some of the small villages in Derbyshire, as a few still have a number of Starbucks living off the land. There is also the intriguing Starbuck House, plus many gravestones to visit!

The Dykes Ancestry Line

You will be pleased to hear that in many ways the Dykes family tree is more interesting.

My Mother's maiden name was Dykes, her father was Herbert Dykes and her Mother's maiden name was Young. Dykes is a British surname, so none of the old Vikings about it, just good old Anglo-Saxon. The surname may have originated from the hamlet of Dykesfield in Burgh by Sands, Cumbria. Other forms include del Dykes, which literally means 'of the Dykes'.

Mostly found in Lancashire and Liverpool, although our branch of Dykes was easier to trace as all our ancestors lived near or around Lambeth, London.

Frustratingly, I cannot seem to get beyond Samuel Dykes who was born in 1782 and married Elizabeth May Dykes (Hill) in 1803. They had eight children. Clearly Elizabeth was extremely well liked as her maiden name of 'Hill' appears as the middle name of all the sons and grandchildren until 1937.

We are a direct descendent of one of Samuel's sons, William Henry Hill Dykes born in 1804 in St Anne, Soho, London who married Louisa in February 1832. They went on to have 11 children (yes 11!).

Unfortunately, the male Dykes family appears to have spent some considerable amount of time in various workhouses in London, throughout the 19th century.

Our direct relative was the eighth son Edward Hill Dykes, who was born in December 1846 and married Matilda on 14th December 1867 at Trinity Church Lambeth.

Now in case your eyes are already glazing over, I have mentioned Edward and Matilda for a very good reason. They went on to have five children; three girls and two boys. Both the boys had to go to the Poor House in Elder Road, Norwood, but Matilda managed to keep her daughters with her.

Stay with me, as the next bit is a little sad. During the 1870s, it was almost impossible to get work. Edward Hill Dykes suddenly just disappeared off the face of the earth. Had he left his wife Matilda and done a bunk? It took me months before I found that in sheer desperation, he had taken a ship to work for the East India Rubber Company in Calcutta. He died six months later in 1878 from typhoid. I could have wept. This left Matilda with five children.

I could even trace the various addresses she lived at, before she finally settled at 4 Cumberland Road, Woodside, South Norwood, just a very short distance from Selhurst Park. She, and at least one of her daughters, worked as a cleaner at the local school.

The house still stands today and I have a picture in my records. She died on the anniversary of her marriage some 58 years later. One of her children was Herbert James Dykes born on 4th November 1871 in Lambeth, spending some nine years of his childhood as a scholar in the Workhouse on Elder Road, Norwood, which again you can see from the Holmesdale Stand at Selhurst Park.

He was my grandfather, who was to marry my grandmother, Emily Rose Young in 1896.

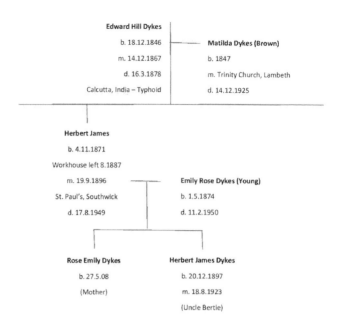

Edward Hill Dykes
b. 18.12.1846
m. 14.12.1867
d. 16.3.1878
Calcutta, India – Typhoid

Matilda Dykes (Brown)
b. 1847
m. Trinity Church, Lambeth
d. 14.12.1925

Herbert James
b. 4.11.1871
Workhouse left 8.1887
m. 19.9.1896
St. Paul's, Southwick
d. 17.8.1949

Emily Rose Dykes (Young)
b. 1.5.1874
d. 11.2.1950

Rose Emily Dykes
b. 27.5.08
(Mother)

Herbert James Dykes
b. 20.12.1897
m. 18.8.1923
(Uncle Bertie)

I have looked at the Workhouse records of that time. They were being modernised rapidly and included a school and also a band. So still not a wonderful place to be, but clearly a great deal better than the dreadful Poorhouses of the 18/19th centuries.

Charlie Chaplin for a short time was at the same Workhouse.

I can remember my Mother saying that my grandfather used to play the penny whistle, so maybe he learnt this during his childhood? However, neither my Mother nor Uncle Bertie ever mentioned that their Dad used to be in a Poorhouse. I guess maybe this was something you never talked about or perhaps they never knew?

Herbert and Emily, before their children were born, moved to a Peabody estate in South London. The charity was founded in 1862 by the London-based merchant banker George Peabody, who set up The Peabody Donation Fund to provide housing for the poor of London. My grandparents qualified and moved to a very nice cottage-style house on the estate where both my Mother and Uncle Bertie spent their childhood.

I have school records of my Mother along with a picture of the house and reports, which still stand on the estate today. For many years my grandfather worked as a postman. It was so sad that both of my grandparents died when I was very young.

And Another Thing

Well that's it really. I have enjoyed writing my book and sincerely hope that there is something for everyone. For those who have somehow found their way through and read every chapter – many congratulations!

However, since I finished the first draft in March 2020 there have been other memories that have suddenly flashed into my mind. So here are a few additional 'nuggets' that you might enjoy.

Long before my driving test (I passed on the third attempt) I had a regular lift to the L&G office with a guy called Fred. One morning he suddenly stopped the car in the middle of the main A23 Brighton road, leapt out and quickly took his trousers down. A wasp had apparently gone up his trouser leg! Life around him carried on as normal but news quickly spread around the corridors of L&G.

When I played the juvenile lead in Flower Drum Song at the Ashcroft Theatre, Croydon I had a small disaster during the Saturday matinée performance. I was meant to knock on the door of my 'parents' house on stage, but someone had forgotten to unlock this door that had just been flown in from the theatre flies. I panicked and shook the door in a vain attempt to 'unjam' it, then had a bright idea and, quick as a flash, appeared as if by magic on stage via the wings saying the immortal lines, "I just came in the back way'. There was a slow roar from the audience, which seemed to grow in intensively as the minutes ticked by. Uncle Bertie was conducting and I remember the tears of laughter rolling down his face, as for my fellow actors well they were shaking with silent laughter. I had thought I was being clever but was reminded of this ad-lib for many years.

Every year we used to visit the travelling fair on the Purley Rotary Field. At quite a young age David decided that he would like to go on the aeroplane ride which went, I thought, at considerable speed with the planes going up and down. I remember watching in some trepidation as the ride commenced – will David cope on his own? Would I have to ask the operator to stop the ride? I watched as David's face changed from the initial 'get me off this ride' to a very happy smile as he whizzed around – Phew!!!

I was the very proud owner of my very own wind up gramophone (1950s) with thick needles as each record revolved at 78rpm (revolutions per minute). You could buy cheap records in Woolworths in Purley; they even had their own record label called Embassy Records. Looking back, some of the unknown singers later became household names.

I will finish with a story about my Mother, which is where I started really. There was a famous musical in the 1960s called 'Hair', which although it had political undertones also included some great songs. It was however really famous for just one thing, there was an element of nudity which had never been allowed on the West End stage before. Croydon Stagers made up a coach party to see this show and my Mother insisted on coming along too. It was a disaster waiting to happen. She didn't know about the nudity (come to think of it, I didn't either) although this actually happened under very subdued lighting. This was the dramatic end to Act 1, suddenly police sirens sounded from outside the theatre and a few ladies, complete with fur coats, stormed in and came up onto the stage to berate us 'the audience' for watching such a show. The only problem was that they turned out to be men, who then opened their fur coats and the rest is history! I remember having to almost peel my Mother from her seat at the interval as she was so shocked by what she had just seen while my Father just sat on the floor unable to control his laughter.

That's all Folks!!

COVID-19

I started writing the first draft of my book in Portugal in November 2019 completing it in March 2020, with time off for good behaviour over the Christmas period.

I returned from Portugal to the UK on Friday 6th March 2020 and almost immediately we went into total lockdown on 9th March. Heather and I saw the spread of the coronavirus (COVID-19) as a potential pandemic and with the situation rapidly developing we decided to self-isolate.

When I left Portugal they had only reported five deaths from the virus, all in the Northern region around Porto and Lisbon, so it appeared at the time that staying in the Algarve region was relatively safe. However, within two weeks of my return Portugal went into a total lockdown which included closing all the beaches. Essential shops stayed open, but allowed only one person at a time to enter, and all hotels and restaurants closed.

Back in the UK the official lockdown began on 23rd March; schools closed and non-essential shops were shut with only those selling food remaining open. Theatres, cinemas and all sports events were cancelled. Everyone was asked to 'stay home' with only trips out to buy food. Three months later the lockdown is gradually being eased as deaths and new infections are slowly declining. Sports events, including the remainder of the last season's football fixtures, are being played behind closed doors during June and July. Theatres remain closed although pubs and restaurants are reopening in a limited form during early July.

Schools will not resume in any form of normality until September, mainly due to the physical impossibility of keeping within current social-distancing rules. This will result in pupils of all ages missing six months of their education.

The first easyJet flight took off from Gatwick en route to Glasgow on 14th June 2020 and, at the same time, our non-essential shops were allowed to reopen but under strict social-distancing rules.

Those over 75 years of age, however, were placed in 'total lockdown' until at least the 30th June. This proved to be the correct decision as over half (20,000+) of coronavirus-related deaths proved to be in this age range, particularly if they were suffering from an underlying health condition. Due to my Chronic Obstructive Pulmonary Disease (COPD) I am classed at being in this 'extremely vulnerable' category. However, the Government has now announced that lockdown for my group will be removed with effect from 1st August as new cases have significantly decreased.

Virtually every country in the world now has the coronavirus to a greater or lesser extent than the UK. The USA has been severely affected and has suffered 130,000 deaths at the time of writing.

A few countries have chosen to carry on as though nothing has happened, but the majority have adopted some form of lockdown. As the virus hit the UK a few weeks after most of Europe they are now reopening borders and taking the first tentative steps to restart their economies. Spain and, in particular, Italy had an horrendous number of deaths; both had their hospitals overwhelmed even though they had imposed very strict lockdowns.

Very little is known so far about the coronavirus, except that it appears to have originated in China. Why it attacks some people severely while others just have very mild or no symptoms has yet to be determined. Clearly it's very infectious and even more alarming is that some people appear to carry and infect others without ever being aware that they have the virus.

The UK Government decided to pay 80% of salaries with other business loans and grants available to help keep business and the economy afloat. Huge amounts of government funds have been spent on many other projects, including the NHS. It is therefore likely, and predicted, that the UK and most other European countries will suffer a severe depression; predicted by some to be similar or worse than the 1920s. But no one really knows at this uncertain stage.

We now live in an unprecedented and worrying time. One day this pandemic will be included in the school curriculum and become part of our history. Maybe you are perhaps reading my book and currently studying the coronavirus as a history project? I am sure, somehow, we will all come out of this pandemic and our country will be strong and proud once again.

Printed in Great Britain
by Amazon